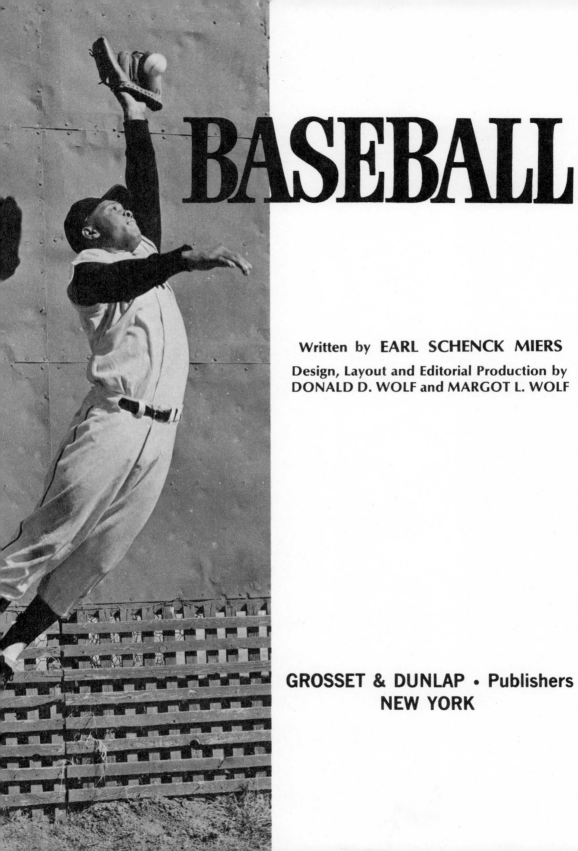

BASEBALL

Written by **EARL SCHENCK MIERS**

Design, Layout and Editorial Production by
DONALD D. WOLF and **MARGOT L. WOLF**

GROSSET & DUNLAP • **Publishers**
NEW YORK

A high leap in the air by veteran
Willie Mays snares a ball near the
outfield fence during an early
spring workout.

Library of Congress Catalog Card No.: 75-112490

ISBN: 0-448-11806-8 (Paperback Edition)
ISBN: 0-448-03367-4 (Library Edition)

1/15/80 pub 3.80

Table of Contents

Picture Credits

An Eternal Boyhood

Zack Wheat! Now *there* was a magical name to lift the heart of a boy growing up in Brooklyn, New York, the daffiest baseball town that ever existed.

Mighty Zack, we called him — this hard-hitting Dodger outfielder whose real name was Zachary Davis Wheat and who had been born on a warm May day in 1888 at Hamilton, Missouri. In thirteen of the eighteen seasons that Zack played for the Brooklyn team, he batted over .300; and in 1918, when he hit .335, he was the National League's leading batsman, though he thrice topped that mark, hitting .375 in 1923 and 1924, and .359 the following year.

No lad raised in Brooklyn during the years of my boyhood ever was expected to have more than three enduring heroes: President Woodrow Wilson, because he was making the world safe for democracy fighting the First World War; General John J. Pershing, leader of the American Expeditionary Force, who was whaling the tar out of Germans for all the mean things they had done in Belgium and France; and powerful Zack Wheat, the slugger who kept alive in Brooklyn hearts that perennial chant of hope, "Wait until next year!"

In those tender years there were still trolley cars rumbling over cobbled streets so that we were all "trolley dodgers," accounting for the reason the Dodger team acquired its nickname; and after the 1920 World Series, nothing that ever happened in baseball — in Brooklyn or elsewhere — could truly astonish any one of us.

If you want to look at the record, 1920 was the season when the Cleveland Indians under the gifted managership of Tris Speaker ran off with the American League pennant. Still, we Dodger cranks expected our National League winners to scalp the Lake Erie warriors. We really never had heard of that Pennsylvania miner, Stanley Coveleski, the Cleveland spitball sensation who pitched three games and won them all, holding our Beloved Bums to five hits in each. What hurt more was when we sent Sherry Smith, our pitching star, up against Walter Mails, a Dodger castoff, and saw our hapless heroes held to three hits while Tris Speaker romped home with the game's only run.

But the fifth game was the heartbreaker. The Dodgers had a man on first and second base with none out. We were ready to roll now! And then the Indian second baseman, Bill Wambsganss, did the unbelievable. Yes, he did — he grabbed a line drive, touched second, tagged the man coming down from first, and there it was, performed right before our eyes: a triple play unassisted! When the shock wore off — and we had lost the World Series, 5 games to 2 — we were immune forever against anything that ever occurred in this wacky game.

If thereafter a first baseman lost a pop fly in the sun and the ball finally bounced off the top of his head, we could believe it.

Stanley Coveleski, Cleveland's spitball sensation of the 1920 World Series.

6

The grand finale of the most famous triple play in baseball history: Bill Wambsganss tags Brooklyn's Otto Miller, standing a few feet off second base. Pete Kilduff (in foreground), rounding third base, looks back to discover that the inning has ended.

Tris Speaker, who managed the Cleveland Indians in 1920, is shown in batting practice when he was still playing with Boston. He was elected to the Baseball Hall of Fame in 1937.

And when we heard that Duke Kenworthy, who played in 1915 with Kansas City in the old Federal League, went back to examine a pebble that made a ball bounce over his head and discovered the pebble was gold, bought the ball park and became a millionaire, we could believe that, too.

And when Gabby Street, who played for the Washington Senators, offered to bet a full season's salary that he could catch a ball dropped from the top of the Washington Monument (and eventually did), we could believe this also, for sanity was not an absolute requirement for success in baseball!

*   *   *   *

And yet, how we loved the game! It was in our blood, our tradition. It was in our folklore when we hummed "Take Me Out to the Ball Game," which was boyhood's national anthem, or when we felt deeply in our hearts for that fallen hero:

> Oh! somewhere in this favored land the sun is shining bright;
> The band is playing somewhere, and somewhere hearts are light.
> And somewhere men are laughing, and somewhere children shout;
> But there is no joy in Mudville — mighty Casey has struck out.

Whether on vacant lots or on crowded city streets, baseball was and still is a favorite game of American youth.

It was in our language, too. "Hit 'em where they ain't," we begged every teammate at bat, not knowing that we echoed the immortal wisdom of Wee Willie Keeler, who once rapped out a neat season's average of .432 for the old Baltimore Orioles. It was in our humor when we read those billboards of the 1920's advertising flypaper: "Last year, Zack Wheat caught 288 flies; Tanglefoot caught 15 billion." And it was in our intelligence also, thanks to the advice that Bill Byron, the "singing umpire," once gave to a rookie: "You'll have to learn, before you're older, you can't hit the ball with the bat on your shoulder."

On crowded city streets on hot summer days, when the horse that drew the iceman's wagon stuck its ears through a straw hat, we played one-oh-cat, not realizing that we were engaging in one of the most primitive forms of baseball known to America. Sometimes we played "hard-ball," using trees and manhole (sewer) covers for bases, and when the ball cracked, we laced it hard with black friction tape. We tapped the bat impatiently against the pavement and cussed silently whenever a game was delayed by delivery wagons or Mamas pushing baby carriages; and when, as ultimately happened, the ball smashed through a window, we took off like rats seeking refuge in a storm gutter.

*   *   *   *

What makes baseball irresistibly the national pastime?

Could the answer be no more than the fact that in its own glorious way baseball became the symbol of eternal boyhood? Perhaps.

But baseball is also a highly complicated, hard-boiled, grimly competitive form of business, as well as a sport — which gives it another sort of status.

After Pearl Harbor, the question was raised in the White House as to whether baseball should be dropped for the duration of the Second World War. President Franklin D. Roosevelt answered emphatically: "If 300 teams use 5,000 players, these players are a definite recreational asset to at least 20,000,000 of their fellow citizens — and that, in my judgment, is thoroughly worthwhile."

Obviously, the game endures because it reflects the American character. But how? Why? This book, really, is a search for the answers to these questions.

Hijinks in Hoboken

Traditionally, cats possess nine lives, but it is far easier to dispose of felines than to exterminate myths surrounding the origins of baseball. By solemn legislative action, in 1939, the State of New York claimed the charming village of Cooperstown as the birthplace of baseball and voted sizable sums to advertise and publicize this "proud heritage" through pamphlets and road signs. An elderly gentleman named Abner Graves, who once had lived in Cooperstown, reached back sixty-eight years in memory to create this legend.

He had seen that first game, Graves insisted, played in 1839

The National Baseball Hall of Fame and Museum, Cooperstown, N. Y.

between Otsego Academy and Cooperstown's Green's Select School. By Graves' account, a local chap named Abner Doubleday had not only "improved" the game, but had changed the name of the pastime from "Town Ball" to "Base Ball." New York's legislators were delighted to take Graves at his word: General Abner Doubleday (of Civil War fame) was, in their unshakable opinion, the Father of Baseball. So more money was raised to build a Hall of Fame in Cooperstown, where baseball's immortals — Doubleday among them — could be forever enshrined for their "incontestable" contribution to the great national game.

In no detail, really, was any part of this story true. Abner Doubleday's birthplace was Ballston Spa, New York, and his early schooling was received at Auburn. On that day in 1839 when Doubleday reputedly was bringing immortality to Cooperstown, the future general was actually a cadet at West Point. Even the possibility that Abner went A.W.O.L. to play as a "ringer" with Green's Select School becomes extremely remote, since Doubleday described his own youthful passions as reading, poetry, art, mathematical studies and "making maps of the country around my father's residence."

Myth-making, an irresistible sport in its own right, even invaded the chambers of the United States Congress, when, in 1959, the nation's

(Right) One of the display rooms in the Baseball Hall of Fame.

(Left) The plaque under the painting in the Baseball Hall of Fame reads: "General Abner Doubleday; 1819-1893; graduated from West Point, 1842; commanded 76th New York Civil War Volunteers from Cooperstown; he originated our national game of baseball in Cooperstown in 1839; presented by the First National Bank of Cooperstown."

lawmakers soberly decreed that baseball "is a game of American origin." Any reliable historian could have reminded the gentlemen on The Hill that practically all ball games had their origins in pagan rites thousands of years old. The ball, in short, was a symbol of fertility, and contests that revolved around it dramatized the conflict between dying winter and blossoming spring.

As these folk rites traveled from country to country, they took many forms. The Persians, who were natural horsemen, whacked the ball with curved sticks in a rudimentary form of polo. Bat-and-ball games were part of early Easter festivals celebrating the Resurrection (the bat represented the Cross), and since it was inappropriate for priests and church officials to be seen sporting about in their undershirts, a game of ball and racquets played behind monastery walls led eventually to the popularity of lawn tennis.

Modern baseball clearly began in England where many primitive variations of the game were played.

"Stoolball," usually played in the village churchyard, was a simple affair: the batter stood before a milkmaid's stool and tried to strike ("bat") a thrown ball before it could hit the stool.

"Rounders," which came next, was a far more sophisticated contest. Now four bases — or posts, in place of stools — were used. When a batter hit the ball, he set off at top speed to circle the bases. The fielder with the ball achieved an out by striking or "soaking" the base-runner with the ball.

Needless to say, grudges developed when the force of such a "soak" spun the runner on his heels. Tempers flared and fists flew. It was not unusual for a contest to end with a tangle of knickerbockered lads flailing their arms and wrestling on the ground in a bloody, glorious free-for-all.

In one form or another, "rounders" and "stoolball" were brought to the American colonies with the first shiploads of New World settlers. As further evidence that Cooperstown was hardly the birthplace of our national game, Dr. Oliver Wendell Holmes once testified that he played baseball while a student at Harvard College in 1829. The game was well-known in Camden, New Jersey, by the spring of 1831; and two years later, Philadelphians organized the Olympic Town Ball Club.

The first book describing the pastime in America was Robin Carver's *Book of Sports,* printed in Boston in 1834. An English woodcut showing youngsters at play at "Base-Ball" appeared in *A Little Pretty Pocket Book,* printed in Worcester, Massachusetts, in 1787, and was copied from a book that had been published in London forty-three years earlier.

General Doubleday, to his credit, never voiced personal claim to the title of Father of Baseball — indeed, there is no record that the General ever discussed the game with anyone. And if modern American baseball *must* have a "father," that distinction clearly belongs to Alexander J. Cartwright, a romantic giant who stood six-feet-two, was as hard-muscled as a blacksmith and wore an enormous black beard.

Alex was a New York City lad who could not wait for a Sunday to roll around so that he and his friends could play baseball. The game, Alex insisted, needed to make more sense, and Alex had everything worked out in his mind: it should be played on a field with four bases,

12

A woodcut, one of the first known depictions of the sport,
shows baseball being played on the Boston Common in 1834.

each base 42 paces equidistant. A game should also consist of 21
"counts" or "aces" or "runs" — but this rule was subsequently dropped.

Various other rules devised by Alex carried baseball toward the
style of game we now know. "Soaking" was disallowed — a base runner
would have to be tagged out, for Alex wanted action rather than
rowdyism. "Three hands [players] out, all out," prescribed Alex, a
sign of the briskness he sought. A chap named Davis was fined six
cents for swearing at the umpire, who happened to be Cartwright.
When Alex said he wanted the game kept clean, he meant just that!

Alex's worst bedevilment was finding a place where his Knicker-
bocker Baseball Club could play. The growth of New York City north-
ward chased Alex and his friends from the vacant lot they first used
on 27th Street. A new field at what is now 34th Street and Lexington
Avenue also had to be abandoned. But Alex was not easily discouraged
— he would find a place to play, even if he had to cross the river into
that foreign country called New Jersey!

Elysian Fields (now Hoboken) became Alex's choice. Nearby was McCarthy's Hotel, where a hunger could be satisfied and a thirst quickly quenched, factors which may have exerted no small part in Alex's selection. The Barclay Street Ferry carried Alex and his teammates to their new gamesite, including a chap called Vail whose inexplicable nickname was "Stay-Where-You-Am-Wail."

The Knickerbockers, under Alex, played 121 games, and none turned out more badly than their first contest on the Elysian Fields against the Jolly Young Bachelors' Club (later the Excelsiors of Brooklyn). The game lasted four innings. A player named Birney scored the one run for Alex's Knickerbockers; meanwhile, Alex's opponents ran up twenty-three runs. How long the Knickerbockers lingered at McCarthy's before they drowned their sorrow over this thorough licking does not appear in the record.

*   *   *   *

Alex Cartwright was a man of rare, adventuresome spirit. With eleven friends he left New York City on March 1, 1849 to seek his fortune in the gold fields of California. Then twenty-nine years of age, Alex loaded his covered wagons with an assortment of bats and balls, for he remained at heart baseball's incurable missionary. Wherever he

Engraving (about 1859) showing a baseball game in progress at the Elysian Fields in Hoboken, N. J.

14

stopped along the way, he taught the game. He taught it in Indian towns, in mining camps and in frontier settlements. He taught it on prairies and on mountain slopes.

Five days after reaching San Francisco, Alex met his brother Alfred, who had sailed around the Horn. Somehow, though, digging in gold fields no longer appealed to the Cartwright brothers, so they soon departed on a Peruvian vessel for the Sandwich Islands (Hawaii). Here Alex happily lived out the remainder of his life, teaching natives how to play his beloved game.

*   *   *   *

Within the next few years preceding the Civil War, baseball gained in popularity throughout the country and America's first game of inter-collegiate baseball pitted Amherst against Williams. The date was July 1, 1859; the site, Pittsfield, Massachusetts. Highly partisan crowds surrounded the field; and an old newspaper report had them standing "five or six deep."

Players were chosen by ballot among the two student bodies. The Williams boys all dressed alike, wearing belts marked WILLIAMS; a blue ribbon pinned on the breast of each Amherst boy was the team's sole insignia. The game began with a heated argument, for the Williams

lads claimed that the Amherst pitcher (or "feeder") was a professional blacksmith hired for the occasion. The Amherst pitcher certainly was a rugged individual: he pitched steadily for three and a half hours!

But in that time, when no one wore gloves, masks or chest protectors, baseball was not a game for sissies. The Amherst boys were first at bat and at the end of the first inning happily led Williams, 9 to 1. The Williams partisans, however, made up in a vocal uproar for what their boys lacked in skill on the field, and the result, we are told, "made Amherst desperate." At the close of the third inning the score stood even.

Midday came and passed; the sun sizzled down on spectators and players as the hours dragged by, but the contest continued without interruption. By the finish of the fourth inning the Amherst baseballers apparently had regathered their wits, despite the howling Williams mobs, and had forged back into the lead. Thereafter the Williams crowd probably wished they had skipped the entire affair, for when the game ended, Amherst had come off the victor, 73 to 32!

*　　*　　*　　*

How severely the Civil War curtailed the game was illustrated by the fact that in New York City alone, during those years, the number of teams dwindled from 62 to 28. Yet in camp, between battles, both Yanks and Rebs kept the sport alive; indeed, baseball was their favorite pastime. And when in 1865 the war closed, Americans rushed back to the far more sensible joy of substituting bats and balls for bullets in working off their grudges.

In America, all sports were more or less social in origin, beginning in colonial times with the tavern clubs organized around such activities as billiards, backgammon, ninepins and shuffleboard. Horse racing, our first "national" pastime, appealed chiefly to the "fashionable set." Early baseball organizations such as Alex Cartwright's Knickerbockers took pride that only gentlemen of reputation were accepted into their fellowship, and their banquets in a rented room of the Hotel Fijux on Murray Street were as important as the games they played on the Elysian Fields.

But the growth of the cities, both before and after the Civil War, tended to democratize baseball. The Eckford Club, named for Henry

16

While the bitter Civil War raged, there was time for baseball in both Northern and Southern camps.

17

Eckford, a Scottish immigrant and Brooklyn shipbuilder, was an organization of young shipwrights and mechanics more accustomed to celebrating around a barrel of lager beer than in a banquet hall. The Mutuals drew their players from the firemen belonging to Mutual Hook and Ladder Company No. 1; the Pocahontas were a team of bookkeepers; and other organizations were composed entirely of clergymen, physicians or policemen. Moreover, fences appeared around ball fields, admission charges were instituted, and baseball, becoming as much a spectator as a participant sport, occasionally found contests ending in a furious free-for-all among rival fans.

Nor could New York City cling to its unofficial status as baseball's capital, once the Civil War years passed. By 1869, *The New York Times* estimated that there were more than one thousand organized ball clubs in the country; and as proof that people "had baseball on the brain," some 40,000 unruly spectators crowded the field when the Brooklyn Atlantics played the Philadelphia Athletics in 1866.

Typical of new teams that were forging into prominence was the Nationals of Washington, D. C., which in 1867 made a three-week tour to such Midwestern centers of baseball hysteria as Columbus, Cincin-

On June 9, 1910, President William Howard Taft added to the duties of the office of the President the tradition of "throwing out the first ball" in the Washington, D. C. ball park.

18

nati, Louisville, Indianapolis, St. Louis, Chicago and Rockford, Illinois, where a 17-year-old pitcher named Albert G. Spalding handed the Nationals their only setback. When the Nationals played the Brooklyn Atlantics and the Philadelphia Athletics, government officials were excused from work to see these games, and Andrew Johnson became the first President to add home-game baseball-watching to the duties of his office.

The comment of the *Buffalo Express* that the next time the Unions played they should "secure the services of an intelligent blind man" for umpire revealed how modern in spirit baseball was becoming. *The Ball Player's Book of Reference,* published in 1867, sold some 65,000 copies. Dozens of songs like "The Base Ball Fever" and "Home Run Quick Step" popularized the game; and the Chicago Excelsiors and the Forest Citys of Rockford claimed "Catch It on the Fly" as their own ballad:

> Come, jolly comrades, here's the game that's played in open air,
> Where clerks and all the indoor men can profit by a share.
> 'Twill make the weak man strong again,
> 'Twill brighten every eye,
> And all who need such exercise should catch it on the "Fly."

The National Association of Base Ball Players, organized with twenty-five teams in 1858, drew representatives from 237 teams to its convention in 1867, including delegates from as far west as Wisconsin. One of the unhappy decisions of this convention barred Negro clubs from organized baseball for the reason that "if colored clubs were admitted, there would be in all probability some division of feeling; whereas, by excluding them, no injury could result to anybody, and the possibility of any rupture being created on political grounds would be avoided."

Fortunately, this decision would not stand forever, any more than would the Association's 1864 ruling that a fair hit caught on the first bounce was an "out." Sooner than anyone expected, baseball was going to become a business — really a big business — and paying customers would exert no little influence upon the manner of game they wished to support.

(Left) James Creighton, one of the pitching greats of early baseball. (Right) A lofty "stand" for watching the game.

The Pros Take Over

Our Merchants have to close their stores,
Their clerks away are staying.
Contractors, too, can do no work,
Their hands are all out playing.

So ran one stanza of that sprightly tune, "The Base Ball Fever." Some shopkeepers fired clerks who belonged to ball clubs, but if these young men were accomplished players, they had no need to worry — irresistibly, professionalism (unhappily, along with gambling) was creeping into the game.

A classic example was the Mutuals of New York, controlled by that notorious political fixer, "Boss" Tweed, who never lacked a position on the city payroll for any player of ability; the *National Chronicle* estimated that New York City taxpayers were chipping in $30,000 annually for the luxury of baseball mixed with Tweedism.

According to Harold Seymour, one of the best historians of the game, California gamblers developed their own style: "Just as a fly ball was about to be caught, every gambler who had a bet on the side at bat would fire off his six-shooter to disconcert the fielder and make him muff the ball." In the East, a shower of bricks and empty whiskey bottles was a more commonplace source of distraction, adding to the hazards of the game for women and children.

Despite the fulminations in the daily press against such practices — any game against the Haymakers of Troy, New York, as an illustration, was compared to playing with "loaded dice and marked cards" — baseball fever continued to spread. The game was changing in style, in excitement, and becoming increasingly the sport of specialists who devised their own surprises to delight the fans.

Pitchers like Jim Creighton not only used the wrist-snap to add speed, as though the ball was "sent from a cannon," but also fooled batters by "dropping the pace," and Harry Wright's slow pitches bore the enticing nickname of "dew drops." Who invented the curve remains a mystery, but "Candy" Cummings received the credit — claiming, according to Seymour, that "he got the idea from watching clam shells in flight."

Fred Thayer of Harvard introduced the "rat-trap" or catcher's mask, and that diminutive Brooklyn Irishman, Dickey Pearce, almost turned the game upside-down by inventing the bunt. The charge that such a tactic was a "baby act" did not trouble Dickey; to score, a man had to get on base, and no one could dispute the logic in this argument.

The father of professional baseball was Harry Wright, and his Cincinnati Red Stockings of 1869 remains one of the legendary teams of all time. "It is well worth 50 cts. to see a good game of base ball," Harry argued, "and when the public refuse to pay that, then good bye base ball."

Born in England and one of the best cricket players on both sides of the Atlantic, Harry turned to baseball reluctantly. He would have preferred to give Cincinnati a cricket club, but he was too good a showman to turn his back on what the public wanted, so baseball was what he gave Cincinnati — paid professional baseball that could compete with "the theatricals" as entertainment — and those who said Harry was crazy and would ruin the game by paying his players season's salaries as high as $1,400 were soon singing lustily:

> Hurrah! Hurrah!
> For our noble game, hurrah!
> Red Stockings all
> We'll toss the ball
> And shout out loud hurrah!

*   *   *   *

And a "noble game" the Red Stockings made of baseball. Their beautiful playing field, 600 feet square and situated in the suburbs of Cincinnati, cost $20,000. The season's payroll for players amounted to $9,500, including the salary of $1,800 that Harry Wright received "by the year" as general manager and center fielder.

But the croakers who bemoaned that bankruptcy must overtake the Cincinnati club soon changed their tune: a crowd of 3,500 watched the Red Stockings beat the Mutuals, 4 to 2; and a few weeks later, when the Cincinnatis turned back the Atlantics, 32 to 10, attendance exceeded 10,000. A large amphitheatre had been newly erected at the upper end of the field, and for blocks around, treetops and house roofs were crowded with spectators. One rabid fan, straddling a church steeple, clung with one hand to the lightning rod while he viewed the contest through field glasses. Wagons parked on surrounding heights spread canvas sun decks to attract paying customers unable to find a seat within the ball park.

For showmanship, no team could equal the Red Stockings. They were experts at the unexpected. Against the Mutuals, for example, Fred Waterman, the third baseman, settled under an easy pop fly, but let it drop to the ground for a double play. And against Irvington, New Jersey, when the Jersey batter struck out, Art Allison, the Cincinnati catcher, purposely dropped the ball so that the hitter must run. Then Allison whipped the ball to second base to put out the runner already on first, and the second baseman laced the ball back to first for another unorthodox double play.

Red Stockings fans roared with glee at such trickery, though rival

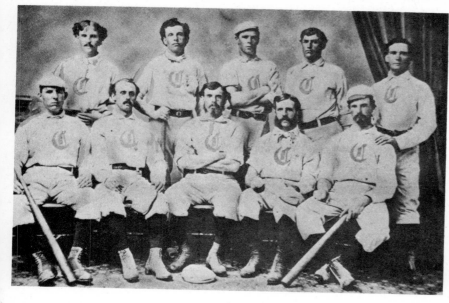

This was the first professional team in baseball: the Cincinnati Red Stockings. George Wright (second from left, standing), was the highest paid player, receiving a seasonal salary of $1,400 as Captain. His brother Harry (with goatee) is the player seated in the middle.

rooters were less than delighted. After the Cincinnatis had visited Philadelphia and drubbed the Athletics, a stream of infuriated home-town partisans, mostly "shoe-polishing boys," trailed after the triumphant Red Stockings, screaming: "Go to hell! Go to hell!"

Before the 1869 season had ended, no one could deny that the Red Stockings were the greatest team in the land as more than 200,000 spectators watched Harry Wright's team play 65 games without a defeat. With good reason the club president, Aaron Champion, crowed to his friends: "I'd rather be president of the Cincinnati Reds than of the United States!"

The team's travels that season covered 11,877 miles, including a jaunt to the West Coast that saw the Red Stockings victorious in San Francisco, Sacramento, Virginia City, Nebraska City and Omaha. Harry Wright, always a "hard-money" man, would not play in any game for less than a $150 guarantee or 60 percent of the gate receipts, and when a Canadian team offered "other attractions," Harry replied tartly: "We are 'not much on cognac, etc.,' and I can assure you we prefer a good game and big gate receipts to 'Hail, Columbia,' 'Won't go home till morn,' and all that sort of thing."

The Red Stockings' winning streak carried through the first four games of 1870 before Cincinnati fell before the Brooklyn Atlantics, a

23

setback that Harry and his boys took in good spirit, even though an over-exuberant Brooklyn fan jumped on the back of a Red Stockings outfielder just as he was about to catch a well-hit ball. Later, Harry transferred his talents to Boston (where he also called his team the Red Sox) and six times his Boston team finished first in the National Association of Professional Baseball Players, forerunner of the present National League.

*   *   *   *

Baseball was changing. In 1870, the year when the Cincinnati Red Stockings began to fall from power, the Pythians, a Negro team in Philadelphia, played the City Items, a white team, and won 27 to 17. The game aroused no ill feelings and the Pythian team was still active in the late 1880's when the first Negro league, the National Colored League, was established nationally. The Alerts of Washington was another Negro team of prominence that issued a challenge to the Olympics, which was accepted.

About five thousand fans attended the game. The Alerts in dark gray shirts, black pants and caps made a good appearance. The Olympics, in white uniforms and blue stockings, had a dazzling effect of their own — enough dazzle, at any rate, to defeat the Alerts, 55 to 4, in seven innings. Revenge came later when the Mutuals of Washington, a Negro club, knocked off the Olympics, 24 to 15. The main point was that attitudes in America had changed: blacks and whites could play in good spirits, without rancor, without recriminations, despite the reservations of the National Association of Base Ball Players.

As a further footnote to the history of the game, mention should be made of the fact that the Intercollegiate Baseball Association was formed in 1879 and included Harvard, Princeton, Brown, Amherst and Dartmouth. Yale refused to join, claiming that "professionalism" had begun to take over the game. This statement (if he ever heard it) must have made Harry Wright chuckle: the Cincinnati Red Stockings, in their most prosperous season, had spent $29,724.87 for salaries and expenses, and collected $29,726.26 for the season's gate receipts, leaving a net profit of $1.39.

24

(Above) "Touch-out at second base," illustrating a scene at the Polo Grounds during a game between the New York and Brooklyn clubs. (Below) A sketch of a game between the old Athletic and Philadelphia clubs which took place in 1873.

And yet, in 1871, discouraging though these figures must have seemed, the first professional baseball league was organized. The time was St. Patrick's Day, which somehow did not seem to fit this un-Irish game; the place was in New York on Broadway and 13th Street at Collier's Cafe, and insofar as "cafe" in those days designated a "saloon," the location may not have been inappropriate. Tradition prescribes that the National Association of Baseball Players was born in a "smoky gaslight ballroom" — a not unbelievable circumstance — where the entry fee per club was set at $10. The Brooklyn Eckfords believed that they were "too loosely knit" to risk this stake, but nine other clubs took the fatal plunge:

Athletics of Philadelphia
The Bostons of Boston
The White Stockings of Chicago
The Haymakers of Troy, New York
The Olympics of Washington, D. C.

Forest City of Rockford, Illinois
Kekiongas of Fort Worth, Indiana
Mutuals of New York City
Forest City of Cleveland

A game of baseball, played indoors at Brooklyn's 13th Regiment Armory in 1890.

26

Silly "firsts" appear in all histories. Bobby Mathews of the Kekiongas, who threw the first pitch, heaved a "ball." Deacon White — his first name was James and he played with Cleveland — led off with a double for the first hit. A fly ball followed, White took too long a lead, and so, thrown out sliding back to the bag, he also supplied professional baseball's first double play. Art Allison was the first man to strike out, but reached base safely when the catcher failed to catch the ball. And the first professional box score deserves its place in history:

CLEVELAND (Forest City)	AB	R	H	O	A
J. White, c	4	0	3	9	0
Kimball, 2b	4	0	0	3	4
Pabor, cf	4	0	0	0	0
Allison, rf	4	0	1	2	0
E. White, lf	3	0	0	1	0
Pratt, p	3	0	0	1	0
Sutton, 3b	3	0	1	0	0
Carleton, 1b	3	0	0	6	0
Bass, ss	3	0	0	2	3
	31	0	5	24	7

FORT WAYNE (Kekionga)	AB	R	H	O	A
Williams, rf	4	0	0	4	0
Mathews, p	4	0	0	1	0
Foran, 3b	3	0	1	2	0
Goldsmith, 2b	3	0	0	3	1
Lennon, c	3	1	1	9	1
Carey, ss	3	0	0	3	1
Mincher, lf	3	0	0	2	0
McDermott, cf	3	0	1	0	1
Kelly, 1b	3	1	1	3	0
	29	2	4	27	4

CLEVELAND   000 000 000 — 0
FORT WAYNE   010 010 00x — 2

First base by errors — Cleveland 4, Fort Wayne 0. Two base hits — J. White, Lennon. Double play — Carey (unassisted). Walks, by Mathews 1, Pratt 1. Strikeouts, by Mathews 6. Passed balls — J. White 2, Lennon 1. Umpire, J. L. Boake. Time — 2 hours.

The Association failed to last more than ten years for a variety of reasons, largely of its own making. Teams that took turns losing to each other in order to create an impression of sharp competition — a practice called "hippodroming" — certainly did the game a disservice. Players who shifted from team to team, responding to the highest bidder — a practice called "revolving" — were another cause of irritation. Respectable patrons were justifiably repulsed by "fixed games" and the *Brooklyn Union* found gamblers operating "more vociferously than an auctioneer on the Bowery." Nor was the competition anywhere near even when the Boston Red Sox could end a season with a record of 71 victories and 8 defeats while the Brooklyn Atlantics lost 42 out of 44 games.

The phenomenal growth of railroads following the Civil War led to the burgeoning of the cities where, surely, there was a growing need for recreational facilities. Yet, by 1879, Association baseball, with no one to blame but itself, was a poor competitor for the saloon, dance hall and minstrel show. Clearly, baseball needed a new genius who could guide its future with a strong will and completely sound business sense. In these hours of extremity, that dynamic personality appeared.

*   *   *   *

Born in Otsego County, New York, not far from Cooperstown, William A. Hulbert grew up in Chicago, Illinois, attended Beloit College, and served fifteen years as a member of the Chicago Board of Trade before becoming an officer of the Chicago Baseball Club. Understanding fully the weaknesses of Association baseball, Hulbert decided to reorganize the game on a new basis — and his methods, according to baseball historian Harold Seymour, were not dissimilar to the monopolistic practices of a Rockefeller in oil, a Pillsbury in flour and a Vanderbilt or Gould in railroads. When, early in this reorganization, he raided the Boston Red Sox for such stars as Albert Spalding, Cal McVey, James "Deacon" White and Ross Barnes, and then hired the sensational Adrian "Cap" Anson away from the Philadelphia Athletics, Hulbert was scarcely a beloved figure in the East. Well could he have told his critics: "You ain't seen nothin' yet!"

Hulbert moved first in the Midwest to form a new baseball organization to be known as the National League of Professional Baseball Clubs. The use of the word "clubs" rather than "players" in the new title gave the tip-off to Hulbert's basic idea — this show was going to be run by *management*. Some authorities give credit for the design of the National League to Lewis Meacham, sports editor of the *Chicago Tribune,* but Harold Seymour quite reasonably leans to the view that Meacham "was acting as Hulbert's mouthpiece."

And no one can deny the fact that Hulbert set up the meetings that bound Chicago, St. Louis, Cincinnati and Louisville in an agreement on the new league. Now came the stickier problem of winning the support of stronger teams in the hostile East. Hulbert drew a deep breath. He was no flincher. He would tackle the devil if necessary.

The four eastern clubs Hulbert wanted were Hartford, Boston, New York and Philadelphia. He met with delegates of these clubs at the Central Hotel in New York City on February 2, 1876, and there is a legend that he locked the door, put the key in his pocket and announced that no one was leaving until all came to terms. His proposition, Hulbert said, "was as old as the hills"; baseball, he asserted, faced "the irrepressible conflict between Labor and Capital"; and he carried the day, for the National League was born before the meeting adjourned.

Hulbert's basic principle of "territorial rights" was accepted — that is, each club was to maintain exclusive control of games within a radius of five miles surrounding the city in which it operated; no city with a population of less than 100,000 — a figure later reduced to 75,000 — was to be admitted to the league; membership dues were to be raised from $10 to $100; players who tried during the season to jump clubs could be blacklisted; and, in similar ways, in Hulbert's phrase, "like every other form of business," baseball's management was to have "absolute control and direction of the system."

Drawing by lot, Hartford's Morgan G. Bulkley was named the National League's first president, a position he held only one term before resigning to pursue a political career that would carry him to the governorship of Connecticut and to membership in that most exclusive of "clubs," the United States Senate. Thereafter Hulbert served the National League as president until his untimely death in 1882.

During its inaugural season of 1876, the National League planned five home games and five road games played round-robin style among its charter members, making a total of seventy games for each club. The admission price was fifty cents at game time, ten cents after the third inning.

The first game in National League history was played at Philadelphia, Pennsylvania, on Saturday, April 22, 1876, with Boston turning back the home team, 8 to 5. Boston's Joseph Borden, who used the name of "Josephs" on the pitcher's mound, was tagged for ten hits in this opener, but would rise to another fame a month later when he shut out Cincinnati in the League's first no-hitter (although seventy-five years passed before historians proved that the two hits credited to Cincinnati in this game actually had been bases on balls).

Not that the National League did not develop a multitude of headaches. Gambling and drinking, though reduced, still spoiled the game for many spectators. Philadelphia and New York, arguing that "the league needs us more than we need them," refused to travel west in 1876 for seventeen games against their four western rivals. Still, neither of these eastern teams, for all they boasted that their franchises contained the bulk of the National League's population, could find much glory in the season's final standings:

	W	L		W	L
Chicago	52	14	Louisville	30	36
Hartford	47	21	New York	21	35
St. Louis	45	19	Philadelphia	14	45
Boston	39	31	Cincinnati	9	56

Nor was William Hulbert, ascending to the National League presidency, intimidated by the arrogance of the New Yorkers and Philadelphians: he tossed both teams out of the League and played the 1877 season with six clubs! But worse trouble loomed: positive evidence disclosed that four Louisville players (including Jim Devlin, the Grays' star pitcher, and outfielder George Hall, the team's home-run king) were "throwing" games at the direction of eastern gamblers. All four players were suspended for life. Devlin, repenting, pleaded throughout his lifetime for reinstatement, but was constantly refused. Finally he joined the Philadelphia police force.

On top of scandal came other disasters: Louisville and then St. Louis dropped out of the League. Hartford, beset by poor crowds, followed as a dropout. Gamblers were willing to wager that the National League would not endure five years, but they did not know William Hulbert. Franchises were granted to Indianapolis, Milwaukee and Providence. The National League, swore Hulbert, was going to live on.

It is living still.

Albert Spalding, founder of the Spalding sporting goods stores, did much to popularize the game as a pitcher with the Boston Red Sox in the early 1870's.

Saints and Sinners

Among the nineteenth-century heroes who made baseball the national pastime, no one really excelled Albert Goodwill Spalding, who would remember those early days when umpires were allowed to delay a game five minutes while outfielders searched in the high grass for "lost balls." Rarely were more than five balls used in a game — a baseball cost over a dollar, whereas a bat could be bought for seventy-five cents — and these facts had an impact not only upon the career of Al Spalding, but also upon the future of baseball.

Spalding was a twelve-year-old kid in Rockford, Illinois, when, quite by accident, he reached up and caught a fly ball hit to the outfield. He was, baseball sources say, a long-legged, long-armed, big-eared boy: a kid still growing. The ball he caught he rifled back to the infield with such speed and precision that he looked like the best ball player in the park. And he was.

In years to come, Al Spalding would accomplish almost as much as any three individuals. He would, for example, become the first amateur successfully to turn professional. He would be the first to take a baseball team on a round-the-world tour and introduce the game into Australia. He would organize a baseball league in England (a failure), create the greatest sporting-goods company in the world, establish a successful bicycle company, publish official guides to the game (and a ghost-written autobiography entitled *America's National Game* [1911]),

31

Roger Bresnahan, the man who invented
shin guards in 1908.

almost win a seat in the United States Senate, and support the completely erroneous legend that General Abner Doubleday was the father of American baseball.

Al's school principal, a baseball enthusiast, excused him at two o'clock so that he could pitch for Rockford. Al was only sixteen when he pitched Rockford to a 29-to-23 victory over the Washington Nationals, then considered the greatest team in the country. Soon afterward the Excelsiors of Chicago saw to it that Al was offered $40 a week as a grocery clerk (a complimentary job), and his days of professionalism had begun.

Al reached his prime pitching for the Boston Red Stockings in the early 1870's by compiling season records like these: victor in 21 of 33 games, victor in 36 of 48 games, victor in 41 of 60 games, victor in 52 of 71 games. In nonpitching games he often played first base — it was small wonder Boston idolized him. Discussing the 1875 season, when Al won 56 games and lost only 5, he said:

"The first glove I ever saw on the hand of a ball player in a game was worn by Charles C. Waitt, in Boston, in 1875. . . . The glove worn by him was of flesh color, with a large, round opening in back. Now I had for a good while felt the need for some sort of hand protection. . . . For several years I had pitched in every game played by the Boston team, and had developed severe bruises on the inside of my left hand. When it is recalled that every ball pitched had to be returned, and that every swift one coming my way, from infielders, outfielders or hot from the bat, must be caught or stopped, some idea may be gained of the punishment received."

A newspaper advertisement for an "improved catcher's mask" of the late nineteenth century.

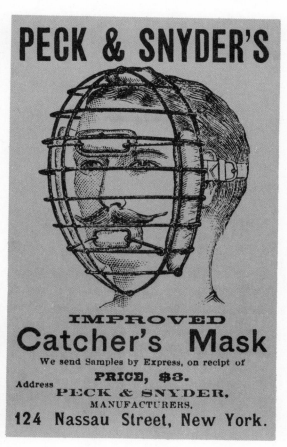

PECK & SNYDER'S

IMPROVED Catcher's Mask

We send Samples by Express, on recipt of

PRICE, $3.

Address **PECK & SNYDER,**

MANUFACTURERS,

124 Nassau Street, New York.

A woodcut from a catalogue of the 1880's. The text described it as a "men's throwing glove without fingers, for throwing practice. Made of oil tanned yellow sheepskin with full padded palm; elastic fastening."

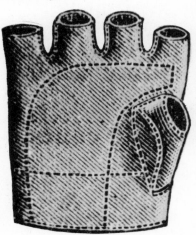

33

Charles Waitt was rather sheepish about his glove, having "chosen a color as inconspicuous as possible, because he didn't care to attract attention"; Al waited until 1877 before overcoming his "scruples against joining the 'kid-glove aristocracy'" and then made no secret of his surrender by wearing a black glove.

"I found that the glove, thin as it was, helped considerably," he confessed, "and inserted one pad after another until a good deal of relief was afforded. If anyone wore a padded glove before this date, I do not know it. The 'pillow mitt' was a later innovation."

The catcher's mask, carried over from fencing, was received with less graciousness than the glove. "Our catcher, James White," Al recalled, "was urged to try it, and after some coaxing consented. I pitched him a few balls, some of which he missed, and finally, becoming disgusted at being unable to see the ball readily, he tore off the mask and, hurling it toward the bench, went on without it." But despite James White, the catcher's mask — which was really the innovation of a Har-

Whether or not "King" Kelly (right) invented the slide, Stan Musial (see opposite page) had his own way of reaching home plate in a 1954 game between the Cincinnati Reds and the St. Louis Cardinals. After crashing into Cincinnati catcher Hobie Landrith, Musial scored, feet in the air.

vard player named Fred W. Thayer, a lover of chess who never walked
onto a baseball field — was a permanent fixture in organized baseball,
along with catcher's shinguards, later introduced by Roger Bresnahan,
who knew nothing about chess but, as a professional, managed the St.
Louis Nationals.

Baseball was growing, changing. Whether or not "King" Kelly
invented the slide — certainly the cry, "Slide, Kelly, slide!" became one
of the most popular in the game — Al believed that long before Kelly
began playing in 1873 "all the varied modifications of the slide have
been well known . . . and, but for the fact that different players adopt
different methods of 'getting there,' not many changes have been introduced, some reaching the bases 'head-on,' others feet foremost, still
others sliding sideways, and a few by a low dodge and grab of the sack
with one hand."

*　　*　　*　　*

The same Rockford, Illinois team that spawned Al Spalding also
brought to baseball the great "Cap" Anson, who was sometimes called

"Baby" and sometimes "The Marshalltown Infant." If there was anyone rougher and tougher in baseball than Adrian Constantine Anson, he was difficult to name, and when later Cap moved on to Chicago as manager and third baseman, it was almost impossible to find anyone in the game more beloved by home-town fans.

Cap stood six-feet-two and looked taller, especially in a coaching box when, chewing on his mousy moustache, he glared down an umpire. His roar, whether directed at that arbiter or a base runner, could be heard a mile away, or so his partisans claimed.

Rivals sometimes nicknamed Cap "The Crybaby" for his frequent spats with umpires, but baseball became a better, more scientific, more honest game for the years Cap gave to leading the Chicago White Stockings. He was a master batsman, once slamming out five home runs in two days in that era of the dead ball; he was among the first to "choke" the bat so he could poke the ball wherever he wished; and that wily pitcher, "Crazy" Schmidt, worked out the best strategy for handling Cap at the plate — Crazy gave him a base on balls.

The hit-and-run play generally is recognized as a Cap Anson innovation; so, too, was the idea of shifting fielders according to the batting habits of individual hitters; and it was said that if a ball came within a mile of Cap's glove, he could catch it.

In 1886, Cap ordered his team to report to Hot Springs, Arkansas, almost two months before the regular season began. Despite the grumbling of his players, Cap believed that the warm waters would help his players "boil out," and in this fashion, "spring training" was invented.

And yet, Cap stood alone, for all his ideas sometimes were called ridiculous. In his twenty-seven years in baseball — toward the end he was known, respectfully, as "Pop" Anson — he had developed a legion of stars, for anyone who played for Pop trained hard and kept in good physical condition. But as the years went by, Pop began to lose his "touch," so Spalding and his associates ultimately eased Anson off the Chicago team, an act that Pop took grudgingly. Yet, over twenty-seven years, changes within baseball, as much as any factor, turned Pop Anson adrift.

*   *   *   *

The monopolistic tendencies of the National League, for all the ruses it devised, could not forever steal "the baseball show." At least fifty cities had developed strong independent teams, not only willing to let in fans for a quarter, but also to play on Sundays, a practice that the National League did not allow. Rival leagues began to blossom like dandelions in spring — and to last about as long. The Northwestern League, founded in 1879, and the Eastern Championship Association, founded in 1881, each endured a single season; the International Association of Professional Base Ball Players, with thirteen teams and founded in 1877, hung on for four years. When William Hulbert died of heart failure in 1882, Abraham G. Mills, who took over as National League president, was equally determined to carry on what many ridiculed as the league's policy of "heads-I-win-tails-you-lose."

Doubtless Mills had heard by then of "Honest John" Comiskey, an Irish immigrant from County Cavan and first president of Chicago's City Council; and doubtless Mills also had heard of the third of Honest John's seven sons, Charles Comiskey, who was destined to outdistance his father as a Chicago tradition and who, at the turn of the century, would be one of the two men most responsible for creating baseball as it is now known. Charles was trained as a plumber, but could not hold a job because he was always sneaking off to play baseball. Honest John stuck the lad on a wagon as a teamster in the family brickyard, but that act, too, was a waste of effort. So Charles was shuttled off to St. Ignatius College and St. Mary's College in Kansas, and came out of these institutions as he had gone in: a baseball crank.

Commy, as his friends called Charles, was hustled off next to Christian Brothers College at Prairie du Chien, Wisconsin, where baseball was not played, so Commy spent his weekends in Milwaukee pitching for the Alerts, an amateur team that allowed him fifty dollars for "general expenses." Commy could burn the ball across the plate and the barehanded catchers of those days cussed his speed while the hitters cussed his outcurve. He pitched Elgin, Illinois to an undefeated season, earned fifty dollars a month pitching for the Dubuque Rabbits in the short-lived Northwestern League where Dubuque won the championship over Bloomington (Illinois), Omaha, Rockford and Davenport, and so finally found his way to the St. Louis Browns. Al Spink, who

(Opposite page) A lithograph depicting a baseball game at Boston's National League Park in 1894.

Charles A. Comiskey in his early years as a ball player.

established *The Sporting News,* the national newspaper of baseball, spotted the young whirlwind of the Rabbits at the psychological moment — Commy had recently married a Dubuque girl and could use the boost in pay to $150 a month, and so his lot was cast with that matchless baseball eccentric, Chris Von der Ahe.

Chris admitted that he was a genius. His interest in baseball grew out of his combination saloon and grocery store — baseball crowds were avid customers for beer and sausages (today called hot dogs). The enormous success of the St. Louis Browns, Chris declared, was the result of his planning, but Chris was bragging: Commy made the St. Louis Browns famous. He could play any position and manage a team with an unerring instinct for getting the most out of every player.

Wiping the foam of Chris's beer from their lips, the fans cheered Commy with virtual adoration. Commy's salary climbed to $4,000 a year, a fat sum in those times, and the Browns whipped just about any team that shared the same diamond, including the then supposedly unbeatable Chicago White Sox.

For a variety of reasons no longer important, Commy moved on to Cincinnati. One day in a bar he struck up a drinking acquaintance with a Byron Bancroft Johnson, a sports writer with ideas that Commy came to like. And thereby hangs another tale — the birth of the American League.

*   *   *   *

"Ban" Johnson (as he came to be called), the son of a college professor, attended Marietta and Oberlin, where he played college baseball and tried a brief spin at semi-pro ball before becoming the top sports writer of the *Cincinnati Commercial Gazette*. He was a square-jawed, strong-featured, impressively big fellow, this Ban Johnson, who took a shine to Charles Comiskey over a pair of beer mugs.

There was little about the National League of which Ban approved — the way it handled players as virtual slave property, toadied to gamblers, and squeezed minor leagues into bankruptcy without the semblance of a sympathetic tear. Ban had written in no uncertain terms about these practices — surely he was carrying on no love affair with the owners of the National League — but Commy just kept nodding: he knew that Ban was right, that something had to be done to save the game. And perhaps all Ban needed was encouragement, for in 1894 he took over command of the Western League (a descendant of the old Northwestern League), with teams in Indianapolis, Kansas City, Milwaukee, Minneapolis, Toledo, Grand Rapids, Detroit and Sioux City. Never far behind Ban thereafter in any baseball dealings was Commy and, together, they revolutionized the game.

Incidentally, along the way, both rose to fame and fortune, but that is an almost trivial detail in this story. Commy helped Ban by managing Sioux City, then switched this franchise to St. Paul, for they were a restless, opportunistic pair convinced that they could outguess the National League at any turn. In 1896, when Connie Mack as catcher-manager fell out with the Pittsburgh management, Ban did not hesitate for a moment: he had just the spot for Mack as part-owner of his club in Milwaukee.

The National League, having grown up in the era of "robber barons," had built-in weaknesses. By 1899 the word "trust" was becoming a hateful business term in the American language, but apparently no one in control of the National League was ready to change with the times. It dropped four of its twelve clubs at the end of that season, and Ban, whose Western League now was called the "strongest minor ever," long had been ready for just that move. He wanted clubs in Chicago, Cleveland and St. Louis, and now he had his chance to move, along with the support of Charles Somers, who was variously described as "a very wealthy coal dealer" and "a Great Lakes shipping tycoon."

Somers helped Ban buy into Cleveland. Then Ban nibbled into the East by picking up a franchise in Buffalo. Commy now pulled his master stroke, transferring his St. Paul franchise to the Chicago South Side — a maneuver made possible, according to one baseball historian, because Jim Hart, who owned the Chicago National League franchise, "never thought fans would tolerate the stockyard smells to see a ball game in that rundown district of town." Commy not only proved Hart wrong financially; he won the pennant in 1900, the year when for the sake of greater prestige Ban renamed the Western League the American

(Right) John J. McGraw of the New York Giants, in 1910, and (below) shaking hands with Connie Mack (at right in the photo) during the 1913 World Series.

League. His eyes were turned eastward toward franchises in Washington, Baltimore and Philadelphia.

Open warfare erupted. Ban played clean baseball — he backed up his umpires, he was popular with the fans. In February, 1901, he was telling both the nation and the National League: "The American League will be the principal organization of the country within a very short time. Mark my prediction."

But Ban was having his troubles, too. Fiery-tempered John McGraw, called by many experts the greatest manager in baseball, did not like Ban's support of his umpires. (McGraw's pugnaciousness had been legendary since that May day in 1894 when, playing with the Baltimore Orioles in Boston, he became infuriated by the ribbing of the local crowd and picked a fight with "Foghorn" Tucker, the Boston first baseman. Soon both teams were locked in a glorious free-for-all that spread to the fans; in the excitement, some overexuberant soul set fire to the bleachers, and not only did the ball park burn down, but also 170 buildings in the vicinity!)

41

So Ban Johnson doubtless felt little surprise when, midway through the 1902 season, the hot-tempered McGraw sold out his holdings in the Orioles and jumped to the National League; Ban simply moved his Baltimore franchise to New York, a city he had long wanted to invade.

Neither league could long afford this kind of warfare and knew it. Player-jumping was skyrocketing expenses. The National League, torn by a bitter internal battle for financial control of its clubs, contemptuous of the demands of players for salary and option projection, scornful over whether minor leagues lived or died, willing to fight with court injunctions or any of the other ruses then identified with the discredited "trusts," could not ignore one fact — it was losing the war. The American League's attendance of 1,683,584 in 1901 increased to 2,206,457 in 1902, whereas during the same period National League attendance decreased from 1,902,031 to 1,683,102. Moreover, Ban Johnson now

Peering through knotholes or over the tops of fences was a sport in itself and an acceptable way of "beating" the price of admission when "pay baseball" came into being.

42

had the American League set exactly the way he wanted — a combination that would endure for more than half a century — with Boston, New York, Philadelphia and Washington playing under the AL flag in the East and ball parks in Chicago, Cleveland, Detroit and St. Louis flying the AL banner in the West.

Figuratively speaking, the two leagues embraced as though sighing, "Peace, ain't it wonderful?" The first World Series game between their pennant winners was played in 1903, and for all that Pittsburgh's Deacon Philippe pitched his heart out through 44 innings and won three games, Ban's Boston club took the championship, 5 games to 3. In 1904, the National League's winner was McGraw's New York Giants, but McGraw, whose temper cooled slowly, simply refused to play Boston, again the American League champion. Perhaps that decision saved burning down half of New York City and all of Boston!

The first World Series in 1903 saw outfielders often getting lost among the spectators at Boston's Huntington Avenue Park. Enthusiastic fans broke police lines and swarmed onto the playing field several times during the seven-game series between the Boston Americans and the Pittsburgh Nationals. Boston won the Series, four games to three.

43

The Brave of Heart

Among the thousands of players who have participated in organized baseball, some have been swaggerers, rowdies, fashion plates, ragtags, clowns, scholars; but among those who truly have won stardom, all have shared one indispensable characteristic: courage. Leo "Lippy" Durocher, who managed the Brooklyn Dodgers, the New York Giants and the Chicago Cubs, once said, "Nice guys finish last," but Lippy missed the truth by the 127 feet 3⅜ inches that separate home plate from second base.

More often than not, nice guys finish first and, if courage is the measure of what makes a hero, should be enshrined in Baseball's Hall of Fame (where, unhappily too often, their greatness has been ignored).

Take the case of Hugh Daly. As a kid growing up in Baltimore, Maryland, Hugh nailed to a fence a tin can which he used as a target in gaining pitching control. At fifteen, pitching for his parochial school, Hugh kept his classmates hopping with delight as he mowed down on strikes dozens of rival batsmen. To help out financially at home, Hugh worked after school as a stage carpenter at the Front Street Theater where, one day, burns received during a fire on the stage caused the removal of his left arm.

Friends grieved for Hugh: what future did baseball offer a one-armed player? But Hugh wasted small sympathy upon himself: baseball was *his* game and he meant to play it. A bat thinned down at the handle made him a one-armed hitter and a good one. A leather pad over the end of the stump of his left arm stopped the sting when he used it to knock down a ball.

Beginning with such local independent teams as the Quicksteps and the Newington Club, Hugh grew famous as the one-armed pitching sensation who could still mow down rival batsmen. From a semi-pro ball player Hugh soon turned into a full-fledged professional, playing with Baltimore, the New York Metropolitans (later the Giants), Buffalo, Cleveland, the Chicago club in the old Union League, St. Louis, Cleveland, and Washington. In 1883, playing with the Cleveland Nationals against Philadelphia, Hugh joined the sacred ranks of pitchers who hurled a no-hit, no-run game.

Almost as unusual as Hugh Daly among the handicapped players in baseball was Luther Taylor, who as a deaf-mute could neither hear nor talk and so was called "Dummy" Taylor. Dummy was 24 years old when in 1904 he won twenty-one games for the New York Giants, helping to win the pennant that year which Manager John McGraw refused to defend against Ban Johnson's Boston champions in the American League. For the next decade, Dummy remained a major-league pitcher and won 116 games. In sign language, Dummy used to dress down umpires, his biggest mistake. One day an umpire, who had happened to learn the sign language of the deaf and dumb, stomped out to the mound.

"Listen," he told Dummy, ridiculing him as a smart guy, "you'll never again call me a blind bum and get away with it."

Dummy, retiring from baseball, devoted the remainder of his life to teaching deaf-and-dumb youngsters how to play the national game.

Other players with handicaps made great records in baseball. One was Mordecai Brown, a pitcher with only three fingers; he pitched in the major leagues for fifteen years and his plaque in the Hall of Fame reads:

MORDECAI PETER BROWN
(Three-fingered and Miner)

Member of the Chicago N. L.
Championship teams of 1906, '07, '08, '10.
A right handed pitcher, won 239
games during major league career
that also included St. Louis and
Cincinnati N. L. and clubs in F. L.
First major leaguer to pitch four
consecutive shutouts, achieving
this feat on June 13, June 25, July 2
and July 4, in 1908

Mordecai's three fingers gave his curves an especially baffling twist. Players handicapped with the loss of toes were Charley Ruffing,

Mordecai Peter Brown (above left) had only three fingers on his pitching hand, which gave his curve an especially baffling twist.

Pete Gray (above right) had only one arm, yet was a regular outfielder and led off the batting order for the Memphis Chicks in 1943 and 1944.

Bert Shepard, who was shot down over Germany while piloting a P-38 during World War II and lost his right leg in the action, is shown rounding first base with the aid of an artificial leg.

Ed Gaedel, a 26-year-old midget (and professional stunt man) was put into a game as a pinch hitter for the St. Louis Browns in 1951. As might be expected, Ed got a base on balls, since the Detroit Tiger pitcher could not readily find the strike zone. (Bob Swift is the catcher.)

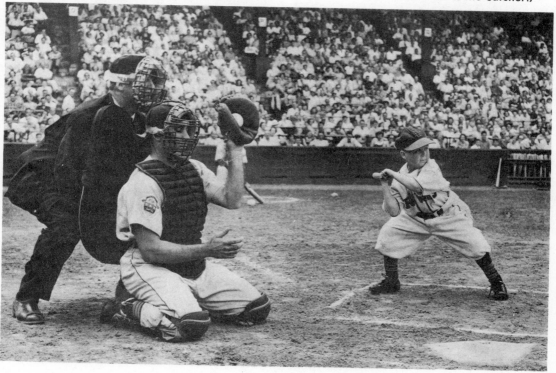

who pitched in the American League for Boston, New York and Chicago, and Hal Peck, an American League outfielder with Philadelphia and Cleveland; one-eyed players who scaled the heights included Harry Jasper, who pitched for Chicago and Cleveland in the American League as well as the St. Louis Nationals, Tom Sunkel, who pitched in the National League for St. Louis, New York and Brooklyn, and Bill Irwin, who pitched for the old Cincinnati club.

Baseball's most famous batboy was a hunchback, Eddie Bennett — players believed that rubbing Eddie's back brought them luck, and clubs began bidding for Eddie's services until he became the highest-paid batboy in the game. Apparently there *was* something to the superstition, for all three teams for which Eddie worked — the Chicago White Sox, Brooklyn Dodgers and New York Yankees — became pennant winners!

In 1945, Bert Shepard, a hero of the Second World War, played first base for the Washington Senators with an artificial right leg. Easily the most ridiculous player in baseball was Eddie Gaedel, signed by the St. Louis Browns in 1951. Eddie, a midget standing only 43 inches high and wearing the number $\frac{1}{8}$ on his uniform, waddled up to the plate with a toy bat; the Detroit pitcher could not find the "strike zone" on Eddie, so Eddie walked to first base and was immediately replaced by a pinch runner; but the next day the president of the American League barred Eddie from baseball for life.

Hard drink ruined the career of Louis Sockalexis, the Penobscot Indian who starred at Holy Cross College before he played three seasons as the outfield sensation at Cleveland; but the taste of whiskey drove Sockalexis out of baseball and finally home to his Penobscot reservation where he died, unknown and impoverished.

Another hard drinker was William Ashley Sunday, who played with the Chicago White Sox. One night, passing a rescue mission church, he heard the choir singing "Where Is My Wandering Boy Tonight?" The song, his mother's favorite, filled Billy's eyes with tears; and right then he decided to change his way of life. So he became Billy Sunday, one of the country's most famous evangelists, who liked to tell the crowds that came to hear him preach, "I'm God's outfielder!"

Perhaps the greatest of all handicapped ball players, even with a polite nod to Billy Sunday, was "Bobo" Newsom, who pitched for just about every team in both major leagues. In 1935, a line drive broke Bobo's kneecap. The next season, hit in the face by a ball, Bobo went on to beat the Yankees, 1 to 0. After the game, the doctors wired up his jaw. Later, a leg fracture at home cost Bobo an entire season; then, kicked by a mule, he injured the same leg.

On August 11, 1907, at Hartsville, South Carolina, Bobo was born Louis Norman Newsom. In 1928, breaking in with the Brooklyn Dodgers, he pitched three games and lost them all; but Bobo, throughout his career, would set some exceptional records, winning 21 and losing 5 for Detroit in 1940. And he would always know why baseball players, growing older, sometimes hurt and hurt terribly, but this did not keep him from picking up the old pill and throwing it for all he was worth.

So, despite Leo "Lippy" Durocher, nice guys necessarily did not finish last, and Lippy should have had better sense than to utter a crack like that in an age when the Grand Old Man of Baseball bore the incredible name of Cornelius Alexander McGillicuddy.

*　　　*　　　*　　　*

Who could play baseball with a name like that? But a wily Irishman, McGillicuddy, changed his name to Connie Mack; and after sixty-five years in baseball — over fifty of them spent as a club manager — that transposed name grew into a legend.

Connie, who was born on December 23, 1862, in East Brookfield, Massachusetts, did not play much baseball as a boy, inasmuch as his after-school hours were spent working in a cotton mill and then in a shoe factory. But in time, Connie — his friends called him "Slats" — broke into the game as a catcher with the East Brookfield team in the Central Massachusetts Amateur League.

And Connie was good! Although he waited until he was 21 before he turned professional, playing with Meriden in the Connecticut State League, he received $90 a month, which was then high pay for a beginner. His debut in the major leagues came three years later, in 1886, with the old Washington Statesmen; and his career would not end until 1949, when he resigned as the nonplaying manager of the Philadelphia Athletics, a job he first held in 1901.

Connie, even-tempered and polite, had few enemies — because how could anyone be sassy with his squeaky voice? But underneath, Connie could be a tricky Irishman, and in *Heroes of Baseball,* Robert Smith, one of the game's best historians, gives an example of Connie's wiliness:

". . . He was clever at imitating the sound of a foul tip by skipping his hands (on one of which he wore a thin buckskin glove) together. At that time the catcher stood three or four good strides behind the plate and often took the pitches on the bounce. But the rule still held that 'a tick and a ketch will always fetch' — that is, that a caught foul tip put the batter out — so Connie every now and then would make a noise like a foul tip, grab the ball on the fly, then grin when the umpire called the batter out. Many a batter was ready to commit murder on decisions like this and eventually the rule had to be changed to prevent the stunt."

Connie was always skinny, as was his favorite pitcher, Frank Gilmore, and the pair became known as "The Bones Battery." Together they moved from Meriden to the Washington Statesmen, but Connie's weakness as a hitter found him dropped from the club after a couple of seasons. Connie took part in the "Brotherhood War" of 1890, based on deep-rooted resentment among players over abuses of the reserve clause in their contracts, limitations on salaries, arbitrary fines, the blacklist and the lack of effective means of gaining redress for grievances. In short, Connie was exhibiting that rebel streak which made him, in time, a warm friend to Ban Johnson.

Meanwhile, Connie jumped to the Players' League, sunk his savings into an interest in the Buffalo club, and saw both the league and team fold up — a fact, many authorities suspect, that may explain Connie's later reputation for "stinginess."

In 1891, Connie, now 28 years of age, started his baseball career anew with Pittsburgh (and he was as tricky as ever, for now he tipped the bat with one hand just as the batter began to swing). A fractured leg received guarding the plate incapacitated him for weeks and his playing days were virtually ended.

So Connie Mack, the manager, emerged — first with Milwaukee in Ban Johnson's Western League and then with Philadelphia in the

Charles A. ("Chief") Bender, famed pitcher of the Philadelphia Athletics.

new American League. Gentleness and patience became Connie's chief traits in dealing with players, and for all the Philadelphia franchise was considered a "white elephant," Connie's soft-mannered methods produced some of the greatest pitchers in baseball history: Eddie Plank, "Chief" Bender, "Rube" Waddell, Jack Coombs, Joe Bush, Bob Shawkey, "Lefty" Grove, George Earnshaw and Herb Pennock. There was no rough talk, no swearing from the Philadelphia bench when Connie was in control; with forbearance he won nine American League pennants, including three in a row. Connie represented one extreme as baseball plunged into the early decades of the twentieth century; the other extreme was represented by that fighting little human gamecock, John J. McGraw, who won ten National League pennants, including four in a row.

*　　*　　*　　*

McGraw's nickname was "Little Napoleon" and a specially built chair in the New York Giants dugout amounted to a throne from which

51

he ruled like an ancient potentate. A "shrimp" during his boyhood days in Truxton, New York, and also when he broke into professional baseball, he packed a giant-sized Irish temper into his stumpy figure.

McGraw fought anyone — teammates and opponents alike. He broke bats. He hid shoes. He was a tough, rough, hard-drinking, mean little guy. He bullied umpires as though under the Lord's command to do so, but he represented *all* the ball players who forged their way steadily through the minor leagues until he found a place in professional baseball with the Baltimore Orioles.

In *Heroes of Baseball,* Robert Smith tells a story typical of the McGraw stratagem as he rose to fame as one of the game's most efficient third basemen:

"One of McGraw's most famous tricks was hitching his finger inside of the belt of a baserunner, to delay his start for home." With just one umpire working, there was always a split second between the umpire's verifying that a fly had been caught and his turning to see if the runner had started from third. Little John just made sure that, during that time, the runner remained anchored to the base. One time Pete Browning of Louisville unhitched his belt while John held it, and when the umpire turned to look at third, there was McGraw with Pete's belt in his fingers, while old Pete tore for home.

When the Ban Johnson squabble moved McGraw into the National League, he went to New York on just one condition — that the club owners keep off the field while he ran the team his way! Nasty, pugnacious, umpire-baiting John J. McGraw was a great manager — a man who took an unwanted rookie named Christy Mathewson and made him one of the most fabulous pitchers of the game — who stole "Iron Man" McGinnity from Baltimore — who swore and raved and gave baseball as good an assortment of pitchers and all-around players as it would ever know.

And with all his bluster, all his abuse, John J. McGraw also could be a kind man, and in heaven two gold stars must shine beside his name.

One star must shine for Fred Merkle, a rookie in 1908 who substituted for Fred Tenney, the regular Giant first baseman ailing that September 23rd, when McGraw's team was playing the Cubs in a game that could have clinched the pennant. In the ninth inning, with the score tied, 1 to 1, Moose McCormick was on third and Merkle on first when Al Bridwell rapped out a single.

Merkle stopped short of second, watching McCormick scamper home with the winning run, but Johnny Evers, the Cubs' great second baseman, noticed that Merkle had not touched the bag. He called for the ball and made the out, canceling McCormick's score! "Pulling a Merkle" became a term of baseball derision that endured for years; but McGraw, instead of blasting Merkle, gave him a $1,000 raise in salary to bolster his confidence.

The second gold star for McGraw, who would start a riot if anyone called him "Muggsy," must shine for his kindness toward Fred Snodgrass, whose muff of a lazy fly ball reputedly lost the World Series in 1912.

McGraw called every play, every pitch, every hit. His base runners became master signal-stealers. His arguments with umpires equalled human tempests. He signalled outfielders where to stand and, more often than not, fly balls fell right into their gloves. And he developed great players by the score, none more "immortal" than an ex-pitcher named Christy Mathewson, who won 373 victories during his seventeen seasons in baseball,* and who pitched three shutouts in the World Series of 1905.

Christy was famous for his "fadeaway," a pitch thrown by turning his wrist *in* instead of *out*. Christy was a quiet man. He neither smoked nor drank. He rarely talked. But at checkers, chess, bridge, at any game of chance, he could not be beaten. Tall, blond and handsome, a more perfect baseball idol could not be imagined; and when he died in 1925, at the age of only forty-five, sportswriter Grantland Rice said accurately: "There will never be another like Matty . . . he brought something to baseball that no one else had ever given to the game — not even Ty Cobb or Babe Ruth. He handed the game a certain touch of class, an indefinable lift in culture, brains and personality."

*   *   *   *

*Walter Johnson won 416 victories in twenty-one seasons and Cy Young 511 in twenty-two seasons.

No history of the first decades of twentieth-century baseball can ignore that sensational infield combination of the Chicago Cubs — Joseph Bert Tinker, shortstop; John Joseph (Crab) Evers, second baseman; and Frank LeRoy (Husk) Chance, first baseman — and the deeds of this trio inspired a verse by Franklin P. Adams:

These are the saddest of possible words:
    "Tinker to Evers to Chance."
Trio of bear Cubs and fleeter than birds:
    "Tinker to Evers to Chance."
Ruthlessly pricking our gonfalon bubble,
Making a Giant hit into a double —
Words that are heavy with nothing but trouble:
    "Tinker to Evers to Chance."

In these first decades of the twentieth century, baseball had become better showmanship. The players — Christy Mathewson, Ty Cobb, who as the "Georgia Peach" rarely batted under .320 and once (1911)

Joseph B. Tinker in 1910.

Frank Chance

Ty Cobb sliding back to first base.

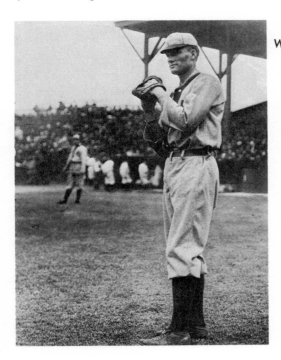

Walter Johnson

Christy Mathewson

55

batted .420 for Detroit, Tinker-to-Evers-to-Chance — became the symbols of better coaching, hitting, fielding. The game was run by managers who also were owners: Connie Mack of the Philadelphia Athletics and Clark Griffith of the Washington Senators. It was run by managerial tyrants like "Little Napoleon" McGraw and by vexatious George Stallings of the Boston Nationals, who in July, 1914, bullied his rookies from last place to win the pennant by ten games and take the World Championship over Connie Mack's Philadelphia Athletics, four games in a row. It was run by Charles Comiskey of the Chicago White Sox, who may have been the biggest tightwad in the business; and by jovial August "Garry" Herrmann of the German-dominated Cincinnati Reds, who called their manager, Pat Moran, either "Dot Irisher" or "Whiskey Face."

Even baseball parks were changing when Pittsburgh built that monstrous stadium of concrete and steel known as Forbes Field, and those who lamented the gradual passing of the old wooden stands with their green-painted seats and gabled roofs wept nostalgically for a lost charm, since club owners were looking for more paying customers rather than sentiment.

True, attendance figures slipped during the First World War, but with the dawn of the 1919 season everyone anticipated palmier days, and the battle for the world championship was enlarged to a best five-out-of-nine game series. That season the Cincinnati Reds, winning 96 games and losing 44, topped the National League with a very creditable percentage of .686; the Chicago White Sox, winning 88 games and losing 52, carried off the American League crown with a percentage of .629. It should be a pretty good World Series, the experts said. What resulted was a disaster.

Homer Davenport, who achieved fame as a caricaturist in the second decade of this century, expressed his view of baseball gambling by means of this cartoon.

"Say It Ain't So, Joe!"

Cincinnati went baseball slap-happy. Its highly German population lifted their beer mugs in boisterous toasts to "Dot Irisher," Pat Moran, whose managerial talents had led the Red Legs to this hour of impending glory.

On paper, the experts favored the White Sox, for in Eddie Collins the Chicago team may have possessed the greatest second baseman baseball had yet produced, and in "Shoeless Joe" Jackson, a Southern illiterate who could scarcely sign his name, the White Sox had an outfielder who could hit in a class with Ty Cobb and Tris Speaker. Moreover, Chicago boasted a good pitching staff: Eddie Cicotte, a right-hander, who had won 29 games and lost only 7; Claude Williams, a southpaw, who claimed 25 victories to 11 losses; and Dickie Kerr, a bright rookie lefthander.

What the experts failed to notice in the lobbies and barrooms of the Stinton and Gibson, Cincinnati's two baseball hotels, was the presence of a pair of unusual characters. One was Abe Attell, one-time featherweight champion and an intimate friend of Arnold Rothstein, racetrack owner and gambling celebrity. The other was Hal Chase, a Giant first baseman dropped from baseball for his frequent association with gamblers; and to add to Chase's unique qualities was the fact that he had played first base for the Reds the previous season.

A crowd of better than 30,000 jammed Redland Field for the opening game. Eddie Cicotte took the mound for the White Sox; the Reds sent in Dutch Ruether, a good southpaw who had a season's won-lost record of 19 and 6. To the delight of Cincinnati fans, who did not know how to pronounce Cicotte's name or whether he was an "Eyetalian" or a "Frenchie," the home-town boys scored in the first inning when Morrie Rath, reaching first base after being hit by a pitch, went to third on a single by Jake Daubert and then romped home on Heinie Groh's sacrifice fly.

Chicago came back to tie the score in the second inning when "Shoeless Joe" Jackson reached second on a fumble and wild throw, was sacrificed to third and scored on Chick Gandil's Texas Leaguer to center. Early-inning World Series jitters could have explained both those runs, but no one yet has offered a clear explanation of what occurred in the fourth inning.

Victor Luhrs, the best historian of this series,* described Cicotte's appearance on the mound in the fourth as "listless," which may be one of the most famous understatements in baseball. Cincinnati's first batter was Roush, who insisted on spelling his first name "Edd," as though anyone would ever believe those two d's, and whose middle initial was "J" without a period to honor both of his uncles named "Joseph."

Anyhow, Roush smacked one of Cicotte's early pitches for what should have been a homer except that Happy Flesch, the White Sox centerfielder, jumped up against the wall and to everyone's amazement (possibly including his own) caught the ball.

There the fairy tale ended. The next Cincinnati hitter, Duncan, singled. Larry Kopf, the Red Leg shortstop, bounced a grounder straight into Cicotte's hands. The throw of the White Sox pitcher to Swede Risberg, covering second, was high and did not force Duncan at second. Larry Kopf beat the relay to first.

At this point everything fell apart. Greasy Neale, who would go on to a later fame in football as coach of the Philadelphia Eagles, hit a pop fly, a sucker catch: Risberg muffed it, though he touched the ball, and the scorekeeper, for no sensible reason, gave Neale a hit.

---

*Victor Luhrs, *The Great Baseball Mystery: The 1919 World's Series,* p. 45.

Cicotte now had runners on first and second who should have been back in the dugout worrying over another year's contract. Ivy Wingo, the Cincinnati catcher who already had thrown out Eddie Collins and Chick Gandil, strode up to the plate. He singled, scoring Kopf. Pitcher Dutch Ruether — vats of pickles would be given out in his honor that night — now tripled, dropping the ball between Flesch and "Shoeless Joe" Jackson, and Neale and Wingo danced over the plate.

In modern baseball, Cicotte would have been yanked out of the game, but in 1919 an "established" winner was not "insulted" in this manner. So Morrie Rath was allowed to double, scoring Ruether. Jake Daubert, singling through the infield, sent Ruether racing home. Ultimately, then, Cicotte was removed, with Cincinnati scoring six hits and five runs; the game ended, incredibly, 9 to 1, in the Red Legs' favor.

Garry Herrmann, the Cincinnati owner, gave an extravagant party that night. He did not know what was going on. But Abe Attell and

"Shoeless Joe" Jackson at bat.

Hal Chase were still at the Stinton and Gibson. And over 29,000 fans, showing up at Redland Field next day, saw Cincinnati (now installed as an even-bet team) take the White Sox, 4 to 2. Again the fourth inning brought the winning runs; among other phenomena, "the ball went through [Eddie Collins'] glove" that day; a triple by Kopf off Claude Williams helped Cincinnati score three runs.

There is a tale of an airplane — a rare occurrence in those days — that appeared over the field at a very disturbing moment; it was said the plane dropped a figure of a White Sox player and this dummy very much upset Charlie Comiskey's team. The figure landed in back of third base.

*   *   *   *

Something was screwy with this series; for a time, faith was restored when the rookie pitcher, Dickie Kerr, won the first game played in Chicago with a 3-to-0 shutout for the White Sox, and an attendance just over 29,000 jumped 5,000 to watch Eddie Cicotte pitch the fourth game.

An error by Cicotte set up one Cincinnati run in the fifth — both teams to this point had played "heads-up ball"; but strange things happened thereafter: a perfect throw by Jackson that should have stopped a run was cut off before it reached the plate (Cicotte, intercepting the ball, had it bounce out of his glove for his second error in the inning) and a double by Neale scored the other run by which Cincinnati won the game, 2 to 0.

The Reds took the fifth game, 5 to 0 — never had betting "underdogs" fared so well. The sixth game, played in Cincinnati, was won by the White Sox and drew just over 32,000. But the next game — won by the White Sox, 4 to 1, saw the crowd drop to under 14,000; the smell of "fishiness" was in the air; and yet, next day, when Cincinnati ended the World Series with a 10-to-5 victory, there were nearly 33,000 in the stands, all bravely believing it had been an honest contest and a crowning glory for the Queen City of the South.

*   *   *   *

Almost before the last fan left the grandstands following that final game, rumors circulated that the 1919 World Series had been "fixed," and Hugh S. Fullerton, who wrote for the *Chicago Herald and Exam-*

iner, suggested that seven or eight White Sox players surely had not performed up to their best.

Baseball, a magazine, scorned the "some fifty-seven varieties of the genus Fat-Head" who claimed that the grand old national game could be fixed; and in a scathing paragraph against those "scandalmongers" who said some of the Chicago players had "laid down for a price," *The Sporting News* jeered: "Comiskey has met that [talk] by offering $10,000 for any sort of a clue that will bear out such a charge. He might as well have offered a million, for there will be no takers, because there is no such evidence, except in the mucky minds of the stinkers who — because they are crooked — think all the rest of the world can't play straight."

But the "stinkers" kept talking — loudly enough to instigate an eventual Cook County, Illinois, grand jury investigation and to rename the Chicago team the "Black Sox" (and sometimes the "Opposite Sox").

Victor Luhrs makes the strong point that a gambler in those years was looked upon as a much more respectable character than he is today. For example, Horace Stoneham, owner of the New York Giants, according to Luhrs, often entertained Arnold Rothstein in Stoneham's private box at the Polo Grounds, giving "official business" as his reason (obviously, for another sort of "official business," Rothstein ultimately was murdered). But the club owners knew, after the Black Sox Scandal broke, that pussyfooting with gamblers no longer could be tolerated on any level. The worst about the 1919 World Series had to be brought out into public view.

The story was not pretty. A great many gamblers were involved — Sport Sullivan, Abe Attell, Nat Evans (Brown), Hal Chase, Sleepy Billy Burns and Billy Maharg — and after the series began, such Midwestern gamblers as David Zelser (Zelcer) of Des Moines, Iowa, and Carl York of St. Louis, Missouri, both buddies of Rothstein, also moved into the swindle.

Chick Gandil was admittedly the ringleader of the eight Chicago players involved — and all, with the possible exception of "Shoeless Joe" Jackson, sat in on at least one meeting with members of this sporting crowd of gamblers.

Eddie Cicotte confessed to signaling that the "fix" was on in the

Opening of the 1943 World Series: Judge Kenesaw Mountain Landis throws out the ceremonial first ball.

first game when he hit Rath in the back. His payoff: $10,000. Unsavory detail after detail emerged, involving "Shoeless Joe" Jackson (his payoff: apparently $5,000); Happy Felsch, who must have made the gamblers wonder what kind of "fixer" he was when he made that circus catch of Edd Roush's drive to the wall; Fred McMullin, a pinch-hitter; Swede Risberg, who contributed four errors to the series; Buck Weaver, who though not involved knew about the fix and said nothing; and Claude Williams, who clearly threw two of the games lost by Chicago.

Anyhow, such was some of the evidence that confronted Judge Kenesaw Mountain Landis, who by a vote of 15 to 0 (the St. Louis Browns abstained) was chosen the new Commissioner of Baseball. The fact that Landis was soon called the "Czar of Baseball" yields some clue to a character that had been known for its truculence, irascibility and unflinching stubbornness since 1905, when Teddy Roosevelt had named him federal judge of the United States District Court of Northern Illinois. Landis not only banished all eight of the "Black Soxers" from baseball, but also threw out, for good measure, Joe Gedeon of the St. Louis Browns for having had business dealings with a gambler.

"Regardless of the verdict of juries," Landis proclaimed, "no player who throws a game, no player that undertakes or promises to throw a game, no player who sits in conference with a bunch of crooks (crooked players?) and gamblers where the means of throwing games are discussed and who does not promptly tell his club about it, will ever play professional baseball. . . ."

*   *   *   *

Was Judge Landis a tyrant or the savior of baseball? He had admirers and critics who will argue either side of the case.

Legend tells the story of the ragged urchin who waited on the courthouse steps until "Shoeless Joe" Jackson finished testifying before the Cook County Grand Jury. Tears streaming down his face, the lad pleaded with his hero:

"Say it ain't so, Joe! Say it ain't so!"

But Joe Jackson could not say it was not so. Indeed, Joe asked for a bodyguard — he was afraid for his life. And like the tearful urchin on the steps of the Cook County Courthouse, there were all across the nation other youngsters who wondered why they ever had made a hero out of "Shoeless Joe," for all that he had batted .408 in 1911 and rarely went through a season without stealing forty bases.

And yet, the man who gave the game of baseball back to the kids of America — indeed, the man who would become the greatest idol the game ever produced — was already on the scene. His name was George Herman Ruth. In fact, he had pitched in the 1918 World Series, winning two of the four games by which the Boston Red Sox took the championship away from the Chicago Cubs that year in a six-game series. (In the first game, Ruth held the Cubs to five hits, winning 1 to 0; in the fourth game, though outhit 7 to 4, Ruth's Red Sox won, 3 to 2.)

In that fourth game, Ruth got his only hit of the series — a triple that drove in the winning two runs. That ball, bounding to the wall, was about to make baseball history. For it was as a slugger and outfielder that George Herman Ruth — the beloved "Babe" — gave baseball back to American youth and to mammoth Yankee Stadium the entirely appropriate nickname of "The House That Ruth Built."

The Mighty Babe

Babe Ruth, the future Bambino, grew up in Baltimore, Maryland, where his father operated a barroom. A loud-mouthed sort of kid — big, crude, a shade above a delinquent — he possessed an oversized cranium which made him extremely sensitive and in later years he could be outraged by enemies who called him "Two-Head." This streak of the "eternal boy" would never desert Babe; throughout his lifetime he was "the leader of the gang" who liked to make up his own rules of conduct.

And yet, right from the start, Babe was a seven-day wonder at baseball. As Brother Gilbert, who discovered the youth, recalled:

"I was at St. Mary's Industrial School one day, and I had seen this boy who, so far as I was concerned, was just a big kid in blue overalls in the beginning. He was catching for one of the teams they had at St. Mary's, and if you ever wanted to see a bone out of joint or one of nature's misfits, you should have seen him, a left-handed catcher, squatting behind the plate. All he had was a mask and a glove, which he wore on his left hand. When he had to make a throw to second base, he would take off the glove and tuck it under his right arm before he made the throw. And how he could throw! The ball was three feet off the ground going through the box and three feet off the ground when it got to second base.

"I knew that with an arm like that he could be made into a pitcher. And then I saw him go to bat. The pitcher for the other side was a tall, lean boy by the name of Tom Paget. As he wound up, he turned his back toward the hitter before he let the ball go. I looked at him winding up and then I looked at Ruth. There he stood, just as you saw him standing at the plate when he was at the very peak of his career. There was determination in his attitude — he had the will to do. Paget pitched the ball and Ruth hit it against the right-field fence. The next time up, he hit it over the center-field fence. The third time he hit it over the left-field fence. Ah, but the fourth time he delightfully, deliciously, delectably — struck out. And he looked better striking out than he did hitting home runs."

Ruth, now nineteen, was signed by Baltimore and was given the name of Babe at the Orioles' training camp. Bought by the Boston Red Sox, he was sent to Providence in the International League for further seasoning and turned in that league's best won-lost record. The Red Sox, bringing Babe back to the majors, never regretted the choice. He won 23 games in each of his first two years with Boston and struck out 118 in 1916. At that time he held the record for consecutive scoreless innings in World Series competition.

But Babe's hitting could not be ignored: nature had made him a slugger. In 1919, for this reason, he was converted into an outfielder, a change destined to alter both Babe's career and the history of baseball. Another alteration would be necessary before these phenomena were completed, and a team once called the New York Highlanders would be responsible for both facts.

*   *   *   *

In 1913, the Highlanders became the New York Yankees for the very sensible reason that Jim Price, sports editor of the *New York Press,* found that the new name fit more easily into his newspaper headlines. Hal Chase, who figured in the Black Sox scandals six years later, then played first base for the New Yorkers in the American League. The long feud with the New Yorkers in the National League — including the opposition not only of McGraw but also of Richard Croker, "the fat cat of Tammany Hall" — now had ended. In the American League, the Highlanders had built their wooden stadium on property running from 165th Street to 168th Street on Broadway, which had proven the flop everyone expected. Frank Farrell, once a bartender and a saloonkeeper, posted a $25,000 check to save the Yankee franchise on the wise advice of Ban Johnson, who privately told his friends that Farrell "bets that much on a [horse] race."

Good and bad managers came and left the Yankees, as though holding transfers on trolleys; good and bad players rode in the seats behind. And so in 1914 the club was sold to two of the most unusual club owners baseball ever would know: Colonel Jacob Ruppert and Captain Tillinghast L'Hommedieu Huston.

The Captain, historians say, was a soldier-engineer who was a self-made millionaire and never had met Ruppert until both learned they were interested in buying the same franchise. The Colonel, by all accounts, was rather a character: a millionaire by inheritance, an amateur baseball player who would not have been allowed on the field if his parents had not bought all the uniforms, an avid supporter of McGraw's Giants, a nose-thumber when offered a chance to buy a franchise in Chicago, but quite overly sentimental about seeing New York have a successful club in the American League.

Captain Huston loved the team: he attended games, fraternized with the players, rode trains with them. The Colonel, with his inherited millions, was standoffish, or, to put the situation at the worst, something of a snob. Yet Huston and Ruppert managed to get along well — swapping managers, swapping players, sharing the playing field with the Giants at the Polo Grounds — until Huston went off to the First World War. Distance seemed to alienate these two friends: Huston wanted Wilbert Robinson, then manager of the Brooklyn Dodgers, to take over running the Yankees; Ruppert set his heart on Miller Huggins, who had done well in St. Louis, and Ruppert won.

Even to see Colonel Ruppert was an enterprise. To find him in his immense brewery, stated the magazine *Baseball,* "you gradually penetrated through one anteroom to another, as though you sought an audience with the late Czar of Russia, when the Romanoffs still controlled one-sixth the land surface of the globe." Uniformed guards nodded politely as you walked through the marble corridors that led from the main entrance to the elevator. "Everything is sumptuously neat," said *Baseball,* "though the atmosphere suggests the yeasty fermentation that is continually going on in the monstrous copper cauldrons." Thus: "You catch a glimpse of these burnished receptacles as you mount the smoothly gliding elevators to the office, and . . . from those same cauldrons eight thousand barrels of beer go foaming daily, with a sudsy current of good cheer, to the huge thirsty city which lies all about you."

In short, the Colonel had money. Poor Harry Frazee, owner of the Red Sox, who had started life as a playbill poster in Peoria, Illinois, had never recovered from investing in shows that flopped. So for an outright purchase of $100,000 and a personal loan of $350,000 to Frazee (for which a mortgage on Fenway Park was put up as collateral), Jacob Ruppert acquired his most coveted possession: George Herman Ruth, alias the Babe.

The Babe never wanted to leave Boston, where he was doing well. He owned a tobacco farm near Sudbury, Massachusetts. Cigars were made from this tobacco with the Babe's picture on the wrapper. The cigars sold for a nickel apiece (perhaps proving that what this country needed was a good five-cent cigar and Babe Ruth, too).

"My heart is in Boston," the Babe said, but he came to New York.

The Babe was an immediate sensation in New York. The crowds that swarmed into the Polo Grounds to watch the Yankees play even included Colonel Ruppert, who was notorious for shunning public gatherings. The power of Babe's bat saw the American League sneaking "the lively ball" into the game a year before the National. ("Home Run" Baker had won his nickname for hitting two home runs in a single World Series; in the National League the celebrated swatters were Wildfire Schulte of the Cubs, who hit 21 home runs in 1911, and Gavvy Cravath of the Phillies, who hit 24 in 1915; and before the Babe

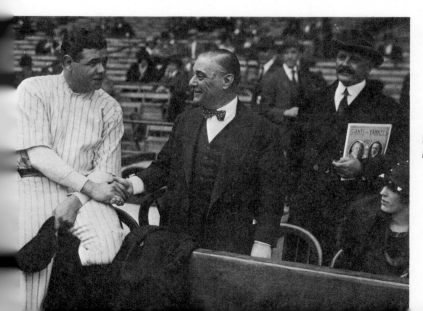

Babe Ruth and his boss, Colonel Jacob Ruppert, during the 1923 World Series.

67

appeared, the American League looked back to 1902 and Socks Seybold of the Athletics, who hit 16 home runs as its "King of Swat.")

Day after day, the Babe made headlines, and his bat moved the pennant-starved Yankees into a three-cornered battle for the title with the Indians and the White Sox (the ultimate outcome was the Black Sox scandal). Ruth hit .376 that season and clouted 54 home runs, but that performance was just a portent of what was to come.

In 1921, the Babe drove in 59 home runs; in 1923, his batting average was a fat .393 and he received the astonishing total of 170 bases on balls. Twice his season's home-run total was 47, then in 1927 he hit his famous 60 four-baggers. As a fielder he was superb.

Ruth's salary climbed steadily: to $52,000 a year, to $70,000, then to $80,000 (and no one could calculate how much the Babe earned endorsing candy bars, sports clothes, cigarettes, cigars, songs, dolls and sporting goods). People who never had thought to go to a baseball game came out to see him sock one into the stands; they came again and again; and when the Babe struck out, they seemed equally thrilled.

Colonel Ruppert constructed the beautiful triple-decked Yankee Stadium to accommodate the throngs as the Babe's team became the "pennantest"-winning ball club in baseball — a structure that truly deserved to be called "The House That Ruth Built."

The Babe who, as a kid, rarely had owned two nickels to rub

Youngster Ray Kelly, mascot for the New York Yankees, gets some expert batting pointers on the field from the Home-Run King himself, Babe Ruth.

together, now "lived it up." He liked to drink, to play golf, to carouse all night (and still appear at the ball park next afternoon as fresh as a daisy), to stay in hotel suites that cost $100 a day, to drive twelve-cylinder cars that could cruise at 90 miles an hour while he sang such old-time barroom favorites as "Tonight's the Night I'm Going to Slug Your Father." Once the Babe's car spun and skidded on a curve, throwing out Charlie O'Leary, a Yankee coach. Frank Graham, biographer of the New York Yankees, described the subsequent scene:

". . . Ruth rushed to O'Leary, lying face down and unconscious on the road. He turned Charlie over, and then, kneeling beside him and cradling the coach's head in his arms, he wailed:

" 'Oh, God! Bring him back! Don't let him die! Take me instead!'

"O'Leary stirred and the Babe pleaded: 'Charlie! Speak to me, Charlie!'

(Above) "The Babe" indulges in some Hollywood byplay with Harold Lloyd, famed movie comedian of that era. (Left) Photographed at the door of the White House in Washington, 1921.

69

Ty Cobb, striding up to bat . . . and running the bases.

"Charlie suddenly sat up. 'Hey!' he yelled. 'What the hell happened to my straw hat?'

"The Babe let his head thump back on the pavement."

One of the nicest characteristics of Ruth, the eternal boy, was that he could never resist a youngster. From ball park to ball park throughout the American League, they followed him in droves. He gave them nickels and dimes and dollars; he signed thousands of autographs, not caring if he were late for a game. He told them what he knew about batting, fielding, handling a glove, analyzing a play. He could resist crippled children least of all. Whatever cheered a youngster was dear to the Babe's heart. He was the Pied Piper of Baseball.

* * * *

In 1927 — the year when Colonel Ruppert raised the Babe's salary to $70,000 a year — Ty Cobb retired from baseball. No other record ever would look so good (except that of the Babe's) as the record which "the Georgia Peach" (Cobb was so named because he had been born at Narrows, Banks County, Georgia, on December 18, 1886) had compiled. Ty broke in with Detroit as an outfielder in 1905, and since then had accomplished these results:

70

Year	Club	League	Position	Games Played	Batting
1905	Detroit	AL	OF	41	.240
1906	Detroit	AL	OF	97	.320
1907	Detroit	AL	OF	150	.350
1908	Detroit	AL	OF	150	.324
1909	Detroit	AL	OF	156	.377
1910	Detroit	AL	OF	140	.385
1911	Detroit	AL	OF	146	.420
1912	Detroit	AL	OF	140	.410
1913	Detroit	AL	2B-OF	122	.390
1914	Detroit	AL	OF	97	.368
1915	Detroit	AL	OF	156	.370
1916	Detroit	AL	OF	145	.371
1917	Detroit	AL	OF	152	.383
1918	Detroit	AL	1B-OF	111	.382
1919	Detroit	AL	OF	124	.384
1920	Detroit	AL	OF	112	.334
1921	Detroit	AL	Mgr.-OF	128	.329
1922	Detroit	AL	Mgr.-OF	137	.401
1923	Detroit	AL	Mgr.-OF	145	.340
1924	Detroit	AL	Mgr.-OF	155	.338
1925	Detroit	AL	Mgr.-P-OF	121	0-0 .378
1926	Detroit	AL	Mgr.-OF	79	.339
1927	Philadelphia	AL	OF	134	.357

Actually, when Ty Cobb gave his 1927 interview, he would play another season as an outfielder for Philadelphia, hitting .323 in 95 games, but that result was unimportant. In 1927, Cobb could give his essential philosophy of the man who faced a pitcher: "Give me the legs of the young fellow I was fifteen years ago and I might make some records." And this, to Ty, was why: "The longer I live, the more batting appeals to me as a mental problem rather than a physical stunt. . . . Batting is a continual study in psychology, a sizing-up of the opposing pitcher and catcher, the observing of a lot of little details. Why, it's much like a study in crime, like the work of a detective picking up a clue here and there."

Babe Ruth may not have believed a word Ty Cobb uttered. The Babe had another theory. He held the bat, usually oversized, low down on the handle. He swung. If he connected, God only knew where the ball might land. When he missed, he swung all the way around and landed on one knee, looking like a fool, but his lifetime record was phenomenal:

Year	Club	League	Position	Games Played	Pitching or Batting Average
1914	Boston	AL	P	5	2-1
1915	Boston	AL	P-OF	42	18-6 .315
1916	Boston	AL	P-OF	67	23-12 .272
1917	Boston	AL	P-OF	52	23-13 .325
1918	Boston	AL	P-1B-OF	95	13-7 .300
1919	Boston	AL	P-OF	130	8-5 .322
1920	New York	AL	P-OF	142	1-0 .376
1921	New York	AL	P-OF	152	2-0 .378
1922	New York	AL	OF	110	.315
1923	New York	AL	OF	152	.393
1924	New York	AL	OF	153	.378
1925	New York	AL	OF	98	.290
1926	New York	AL	OF	152	.372
1927	New York	AL	OF	151	.356
1928	New York	AL	OF	154	.323
1929	New York	AL	OF	135	.345
1930	New York	AL	P-OF	145	1-0 .359
1931	New York	AL	OF	145	.373
1932	New York	AL	OF	132	.341
1933	New York	AL	P-OF	137	1-0 .301
1934	New York	AL	OF	125	.288
1935	Boston	NL	OF	28	.181

Nobody loved the Babe better than his friends — particularly those friends who knew what was wrong. Look at the record and what does it mean? That an oversized boy out of Baltimore had thrown his

Babe Ruth at bat.

(Right) The "Bambino" makes his farewell appearance before devoted fans.

(Far right) Casket containing body of Babe Ruth is carried into Yankee Stadium ("The House That Ruth Built") to lie in state.

money away on friends, had lost his talent, and now had gone wrong? It was difficult to judge this guy who, heckled by a hostile mob in Chicago, once had pointed his finger toward the fence as though saying, "There, by the spirit of good Brother Gilbert, I will hit the next ball," and over that exact spot in the fence the ball had sailed. Thousands cheered. Thousands always did.

But not one in ten million Americans knew the real Babe Ruth.

*   *   *   *

Friends began to worry about the Babe's future. His legs could not forever keep their bounce: age was the invincible foe of all ball players. Finally Babe, the big spender, was persuaded to invest some of his money in annuities as an insurance against his declining years.

Babe, who could not manage himself, broke with the New York Yankees when the owners would not name him as manager. A final season followed with the Boston Braves in the National League as an assistant manager and first baseman. But the old Babe was nearing the end of the trail; yet his last game, played against Pittsburgh, added to the Ruth legend — the Babe hit three home runs in that game. Old-timers insist to this day that his third four-bagger was the longest clout ever seen at Forbes Field.

The Babe failed to gain the managership of the Brooklyn Dodgers, but greater tragedy awaited the immortal Bambino. Severe pains in the neck were the first indication of his cancer. His fine body shrank to a mere shadow. He was in and out of hospitals. When he tried to speak to reporters, his voice failed. Tears ran down his cheeks. He made one last appearance at Yankee Stadium. He wore his old uniform — number 3 — which is preserved now in the Hall of Fame at Cooperstown. He tried to speak; a mere echo was all he could manage.

The fans were on their feet, cheering, crying, their hearts overflowing with love for this walking dead man. The Old Babe! Who ever before had equalled him? Who ever would or could?

With a thin smile Ruth turned on his shrunken legs and shuffled back to the dugout. He had said his farewell to the living — at the Stadium, across the country, around the world. No tribute to the Babe has captured so well his meaning than a single sentence in a short sketch by Robert Smith:

". . . During World War II, the Japanese who taunted our marines in the jungles of the Pacific could think of no more bitter insult to hurl against our flag than: 'To hell with Babe Ruth!' "

The plaque in the Baseball Hall of Fame dedicated to George Herman (Babe) Ruth.

75

Frills and Thrills (and Cheers and Tears)

Bill Terry

Joe Cronin

Anyone can argue that one game or another was baseball's most exciting performance, but, among experts, most such discussions begin with the All-Star Game of 1934. This series, really the creation of Arch Ward, sports editor of the *Chicago Tribune* (who also had initiated football's annual game between the top college players and the best professional team), had started the year before — and it had surprised no one when the American League had won this first All-Star Game, 4 to 2, on a two-run homer by Babe Ruth.

The Nationals were hungry for revenge in the second game played in New York City on July 10, 1934. A crowd of 48,363 jammed their way into the park that day and paid a total of $52,982 to witness what forever afterward would be known as the "dream game."

Joe Cronin of Washington managed the American League All Stars; Bill Terry of the New York Giants managed the Nationals.

At the Polo Grounds, up on Coogan's Bluff, rabid National fans talked with what little sense they retained (which was not much) about a 31-year-old pitcher named Carl Owen Hubbell. Carl's birthplace was Carthage, Missouri; he had broken into the majors with the Giants in 1928, winning 10 and losing 6 in 20 games pitched; thereafter, his won-lost records had read 18-11, 17-12, 14-12, 18-11, until in 1933 he had accumulated a very creditable record of 23-12. That year Hubbell won two World Series games for the Giants, who had beaten Washington, 4 games to 1.

Hubbell was a left-hander and his specialty was the screwball, which, as its name suggested, could be an erratic pitch. Moreover, the Polo Grounds was a short-distance ball park where a homer was easily hit. If Bill Terry broke out into an early sweat, no one blamed him. Carl walked Heinie Manush of the Senators, the first batter to face him. Charlie Gehringer of Detroit singled and Heinie went to second.

And now, one by one, they came up to the plate, the Murderer's Row of the American League.

First appeared the Babe.

The afternoon was warm — and so was Carl Hubbell's screwball — and after three mighty swings the Babe walked back to the dugout, shaking his head in befuddlement. But Manush and Gehringer executed a perfect double steal on that third pitch. Carl Hubbell reached for the resin bag, then wiped the sweat off his face.

Like a clown, Manush hopped down and up the third base line. Hubbell glanced briefly at him and then looked long at the next batter — the great Lou Gehrig, Yankee first baseman, whose batting averages in the past four years had read .379, .341, .349, .334. Hub went back to the resin bag, squeezed it once more, and then uncorked his screwball. Three times Lou swung mightily, and then, like Ruth, tramped back to the dugout, shaking his head.

But now up to the plate came Philadelphia's Jimmy Foxx — Jimmy, who had hit .364 in 1932 and .356 the following season, and who stood next to the Babe as the American League's home-run slugger. Hub's deep breath was honestly forgivable now — not because Manush, like a monkey on a stick, kept dancing along that third base line — but because Jimmy was nothing less than potential dynamite. Two years ago, Jimmy Foxx had hit 58 home runs.

The screwball sizzled and sank. Foxx went down, swinging.

Cheers almost tore the sides off Coogan's Bluff, and then a strange thing happened. A silence fell over the Polo Grounds, so profound that everyone knew what it meant, when Hub walked out to the mound for the second inning.

First up to the plate strode Chicago's Al Simmons (actually, his name was Aloysius Szymanski); he had played for Philadelphia as an outfielder in 1931 and 1932, hitting .390 and .322; and in 1933, his first season with the White Sox, he had banged out a neat .331, some of his hits being balls that had bounced off the fence.

Hub looked at Simmons coolly, then struck him out!

Joe Cronin came striding out of the batter's circle — Irish Joe, manager-shortstop of Washington's un-Irish Senators in those years — and no mean hitter, either: .318 in 1932, .309 in 1933. Hub pitched him the screwball and that made it complete — Murderer's Row, struck down, five in a chain!

Of course, the charm did not go on forever — even though Joe Medwick and Frankie Frisch contributed home runs to the valiant National League effort, the Americans won, 9 to 7. Mel Harder of Cleveland was given credit for the victory; Van Mungo of the Brooklyn Dodgers took the loss. But the memory, the miracle, of the game was Hub's strike-out of Murderer's Row.

*   *   *   *

Who, really, can name baseball's most unforgettable moment? It was on the last day of the 1927 season that the Babe hit his 60th homer — now *there* was a moment. And there was a day in 1941 when Joe DiMaggio hit successfully in his 56th consecutive game — and *that,* too, was a moment. And there was another moment, occurring in early October of 1947, that deserves the description of Red Smith, who as a sports writer became to baseball what Thomas Jefferson, as a statesman-scrivener, meant to the Declaration of Independence:

". . . At the risk of shattering this gazette's [the *New York Herald-Tribune's*] reputation for probity, readers are asked to believe that these things happened in Ebbets Field:

"After 136 pitches, Floyd Bevens, of the Yankees, had the only no-hit game ever played in a World Series. But he threw 137 pitches and lost, 3 to 2.

"With two out in the ninth inning, a preposterously untidy box score showed one run for the Dodgers, no hits, ten bases on balls, seven men left on base, and two more aboard waiting to be left. There still are two out in the ninth. . . .

Jimmy Foxx.

Joe Medwick, in the 1941 World Series, was still a top ball player —on the field as well as at bat. Here he is shown leaning over a four-foot wall, 402 feet from home plate, making a spectacular catch that robbed Joe DiMaggio of the Yanks of a home run.

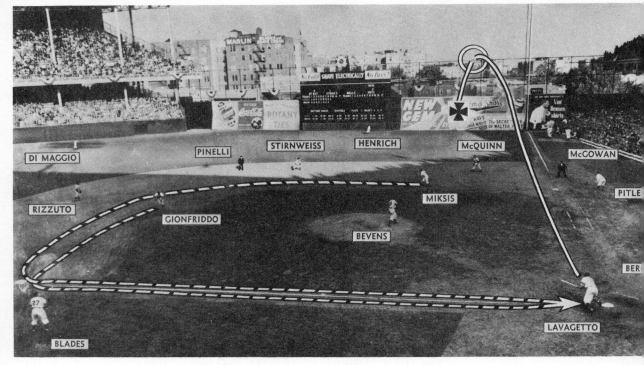

In one of the most exciting moments of baseball, Cookie Lavagetto, pinch-hitting for the Brooklyn Dodgers in the ninth inning of the fourth game of the 1947 World Series, connected for a shattering two-bagger that simultaneously spoiled Bill Bevens' imminent no-hitter and drove in the tying and winning runs.

"In the ninth, [John] Lindell pressed his stern against the left-field fence and caught a smash by Bruce Edwards. Jake Pitler, coaching for the Dodgers at first base, flung his hands aloft and his cap to the ground.

"And finally, Bucky Harris, who has managed major-league teams in Washington, Detroit, Boston, Philadelphia and New York, violated all ten commandments of the dugout by ordering Bevens to walk Peter Reiser and put the winning run on base.

"[Cookie] Lavagetto, who is slightly less experienced than Harris, then demonstrated why this maneuver is forbidden in the managers' guild.

"Cookie hit the fence. A character named Al Gionfriddo ran home. Running, he turned and beckoned frantically to a character named Eddie Miksis. Eddie Miksis ran home.

"Dodgers pummeled Lavagetto. Gionfriddo and Miksis pummeled each other. Cops pummeled Lavagetto. Ushers pummeled Lavagetto. Ushers pummeled one another. Three soda butchers in white caps ran onto the field and threw forward passes with their white caps. In the tangle Bevens could not be seen.

"The unhappiest man in Brooklyn is sitting up here now in the far end of the press box. The 'v' on his typewriter is broken. He can't write either Lavagetto or Bevens."

Who were they, these men who flirted with baseball immortality? Floyd Clifford Bevens — his nickname was Bill — pitched four seasons with the Yankees (1944-47), and these were his won-lost averages: 4-1, 13-9, 16-13, 7-13. Harry Arthur (Cookie) Lavagetto, born in Oakland, California, on December 1, 1914, and playing three seasons with Pittsburgh before moving to Brooklyn, had only hit .300 once in his lifetime (1939). So despite Red Smith, Bucky Harris was not breaking the ten commandments of the dugout — Reiser, whom he ordered walked, had hit .309 that season: Reiser was by far the greater threat. Maybe what all these figures amount to is the simple observation that the game is run by nuts for other nuts to enjoy.

*   *   *   *

Baseball's one hundredth anniversary was observed in 1939. The year began sadly. Colonel Jacob Ruppert — the man who brought Ruth and Huggins, Joe McCarthy and Joe DiMaggio into baseball, and made the New York Yankees so great a club, many believed professional baseball could not endure unless the team were broken up* — died that year. Ruppert's funeral in St. Patrick's Cathedral was attended by baseball's and the city's notables, and, reading his obituaries, as Frank Graham has observed, fans suddenly felt close to this genius who, rarely leaving his brewery, had never married. That centennial year, 1939, would also see the Hall of Fame dedicated at Cooperstown and the United States Government issuing a special postage stamp honoring baseball as the national pastime. One could remember little side issues:

---

*Beginning in 1926, the Yankees won the American League pennant in 1927, 1928, 1932, 1936, 1937, 1938, 1939; they won the World Series in 1927 (4-0), in 1928 (4-0), in 1932 (4-0), in 1936 (4-2), in 1937 (4-1), in 1938 (4-0), in 1939 (4-0).

(Above left) "Iron Man" Lou Gehrig steps up to the plate for his 1,600th league game. The date was August 8, 1935, and he and his Yankee teammates were playing against the Athletics. (Above) Robert "Red" Rolfe and Joe DiMaggio of the Yankees advance as Lou Gehrig flies out to right field in the sixth game of the 1936 World Series. (The Yankees were playing the Giants.) (Left) Lou wipes a tear from his eye as he bids farewell to the fans in April, 1939. (Below) Joe McCarthy holds a plaque dedicated to the memory of Lou Gehrig. Lou's parents are seated in the box.

Charlie Keller, nicknamed "King Kong" because Lefty Gomez described him as "the first ball player brought back alive by Frank Buck," came up to the Yankees that year.

And then there was Lou Gehrig. Lou, the Yankee first baseman, had joined the Yankees as a regular in 1925. He would hit under .300 only twice — in 1925, his first full year, and in 1938, his last full year, when his average would be the same: .295. Meanwhile, Lou was the most "hip" guy on the Yankees. He hit homers right behind the Babe — and almost as many. He would play, consecutively, 2,130 games.

In 1938, when Lou began to slow down — he hit 29 home runs that season, great for most players, but not up to Lou's best — the team pretended not to notice. Lou's legs were slow — all his movements were slow. At spring training in 1939, Lou performed badly; he tried — oh,

Lord, how he tried! — but the old snap was gone. He played eight games in 1939 before he walked into Manager McCarthy's office.

"I'm benching myself, Joe," he said.

McCarthy tried to make the question sound light-hearted: "Why?"

"For the good of the team," Lou answered. He spoke solemn, honest words: "I just can't seem to get going."

Lou went to the Mayo Clinic in Rochester, Minnesota. The report was grim: Lou was afflicted with "amyotrophic lateral sclerosis" — in lay terms, a chronic form of infantile paralysis. The verdict was dreadful: "Mr. Gehrig will be unable to continue his active participation as a baseball player, inasmuch as it is advisable that he conserve his muscular energy."

In short, Lou had been handed a death sentence.

Who could talk about it?

Who wanted to remember that in his 1,000th game, Lou had enjoyed a perfect day at bat, getting three for three, including two doubles?

Who wanted to remember that in his 1,500th game, played at Shibe Park in Philadelphia, doting fans who called him the "Old Iron Horse" had cheered wildly when Lou had smacked out his 48th home run of the season?

Who wanted to remember that in his 2,000th game, his lone hit, a single, sent one runner (Red Rolfe) across the plate and placed the youngest star in the Yankee firmament, Joe DiMaggio, in scoring position?

Lou through? It could *not* be true.

Players, sports writers, if they could discuss the subject at all, tried to joke about it. But the truth had to prevail and on July 4th of that centennial year, in Yankee Stadium, they held Gehrig Appreciation Day.

A big town that was not supposed to contain an ounce of sentiment forgot itself. Anyone who could crowd into the Stadium was there that Independence Day. Fat little Mayor Fiorello H. LaGuardia appeared in a sweat. And Postmaster Jim Farley, who had issued the postage stamp honoring baseball. And so many Yankee "greats," they were hard to count: The Babe, Bob Meusel, Herb Pennock, Waite Hoyt . . . a long list.

And Wally Pipp, from whom Lou had taken over the job as Yankee first baseman.

And Lou's wife, Eleanor, and his mother and father. There were a lot of speeches, but only one that mattered.

Before this great Yankee team that would win 106 games and lose 45, taking the pennant by a margin of seventeen games, stepped Lou. Shortly he would be dead, but that did not mean anything now. He spoke slowly, saying, "I consider myself the luckiest man on the face of this earth."

And baseball, then a hundred years old, would live to be a thousand years old, as long as it remembered Lou Gehrig.

*　　*　　*　　*

Three years before Lou Gehrig retired from the game, modern night baseball was started in 1935 by Larry McPhail, who then was leader of the Cincinnati Reds. President Franklin D. Roosevelt, sitting in the White House, pressed a button that turned on the lights at Crosley Field. Later, as McPhail moved along in his colorful career, first as president of the Brooklyn Dodgers and then of the New York Yankees, he would install high-level lighting. In time, only one club would refuse to succumb to McPhail's fad — the Chicago Cubs. They still do.

Really, it was never McPhail's fad — night baseball went as far back as 1880 when, with the aid of arc lights stretched along the field, two amateur teams on Massachusetts' Nantucket Island tried to finish a game by 9:30 P.M. There is a record that Quincy, Illinois, beat Fort Wayne, Indiana, by the awful score of 19 to 11 in a night game on June 2, 1883; and, apparently, early in the twentieth century, night games were played in Baltimore, Maryland, and Wilmington, Delaware; and in 1929, investing $19,000 in lights, the Des Moines, Iowa team announced that it would play its games at night. A rival club, Independence, Kansas, deprived Des Moines of this distinction by stringing up arc lights for a game against Lincoln, Nebraska, three days (nights) earlier.

When McPhail carried the major leagues into night-time business, each club was limited to seven evening affairs; then, as though shooting

dice, the club owners increased night games in a sequence of seven —
to 14, then 21 (for Washington, D.C.). The minor leagues grew deliri-
ous — night baseball was saving them from bankruptcy. So more and
more lights were turned on. Did it make a difference? Joe DiMaggio
once told Willie Mays that playing under the arcs had shortened his
playing career by three years. Willie, who had grown up with night
baseball, could not see where the lights had made any change in his
playing.

But baseball was always changing, and even Willie would discover
this fact in time.

*   *   *   *

The first Ladies Day — if you can believe the story — occurred
in 1897. The owners of the Washington Senators were the sponsors.
On this "free day" for the ladies the attraction was George Mercer,
a pitcher and handsome devil called "Winnie." Apparently, Winnie
did not like the umpire, Bill Carpenter. In the fifth inning Winnie
strode down from the mound and offered Mr. Carpenter a pair of eyeglasses, after which Winnie, not unexpectedly, was requested to leave
the scene of action. What happened thereafter is the responsibility of
Marc Davis, who tells this yarn in a book called *Baseball's Unfor-
gettables:*

"Most of the women in the stands jumped to their feet and screeched
their hatred at the umpire. But he ignored their wrath, and the game
proceeded without their glamorous hero, Winnie Mercer, on the mound.

"But no sooner was the game over than thousands of infuriated
females poured out of the stands, shouting threats at the umpire. Where-
upon the brave arbiter who never had quailed before the fury of a male
mob now became frightened and hastened to cover. Before he could
reach the safety of the Washington club house, several women attacked
him and tore his clothes. Once inside, Umpire Carpenter demanded that
the Washington club protect him. So, they bolted the doors and closed
the heavy window shutters, as a hail of stones and bricks crashed against
the structure. Many of the enraged women used their parasols to beat
against the shutters. Some even found clubs with which they tried to
break down the door. Another horde of angry females began to vent

their rage on the ball park. Seats were ripped out, windows were broken, and railings bent. The police were called, but the women continued. They remained in the ball park until dark, waiting for the umpire. Meanwhile, the frightened arbiter had to be smuggled out of the ball park, to save his life."

Other sources cite June 16, 1883, as the date of the first Ladies Day in a game played between the Giants and Cleveland at the Polo Grounds; there is no mention of a riot. The St. Louis Browns tried regular Ladies Days in 1912, stipulating that each woman must be accompanied by a gentleman; but insofar as throngs of females loitered near the gates, trying to obtain male escorts, the Browns' management could not always be certain the term "ladies" fitted this group. But Ladies Day persisted, and became more or less a permanent part of baseball after Branch Rickey, who then bossed the Cards, instituted them as a St. Louis custom in 1917.

* * * *

Since sooner or later the pages of this chronicle must add the story of the umpire, perhaps the recollection of the female admirers of Winnie Mercer beating with their parasols on the shutters of the club-house while the arbiter of that game cowered behind a bolted door offers an appropriate opening. A sign posted in a Kansas City ball park some

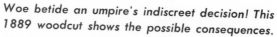
Woe betide an umpire's indiscreet decision! This 1889 woodcut shows the possible consequences.

(Left) Is the foot on or off the bag? Instructor shows trainees what to look for at Umpire School, Cocoa, Florida.

(Opposite page) Umpire Art Passarella called Yankee runner Johnny Sain out in a play that took place in the tenth inning of the fifth World Series game between the Dodgers and the Yankees (1955). Despite the subsequent vehement protest by coach Bill Dickey (33), the call stood. The picture as caught by high-speed camera would indicate that the decision was wrong. (Far right) Leo "The Lip" Durocher registers one of the many protests of his career.

eleven years earlier, "Please do not shoot the umpire. He is doing the best he can," might have calmed down the Washington ladies.

Actually, the history of "the men in blue" — or, as sportscaster Russ Hodges has called them, "the men in boo" — begins in baseball's earliest years. The umpire was, legend tells us, a dignified fellow who, occupying a high stool midway down the base line between home and first, wore a Prince Albert coat. Such aloofness apparently was not enough; primitive baseball yarns tell of umpires being tarred and feathered.

As early as 1871, the rules of organized baseball provided that no appeal could be made from an umpire's judgment (the rules, unhappily, applied to the players and not the fans); in 1882, an umpire, Richard Higham, was expelled for dishonesty; and in the first days of the National League, an ex-prizefighter, William B. McLean, doubtless deserved his nickname of "King of Umpires," for this Philadelphian demanded that arbiters be paid for their services — $5 a game.

In 1883, the American Association, making umpires employees of the league, paid them $140 a month "plus traveling expenses and hotel bills, not to exceed $3 a day"; and Ban Johnson, backing up his umpires with such firmness that he drove scrappy John J. McGraw out of the new American League, finally gave full dignity to the men in blue. About this time a second umpire was added to the game, with the man

behind the plate designated the umpire-in-chief. Thirty more years would pass before the majors added four umpires for regular contests and six umpires for World Series games.

Bill Klem, called "The Old Arbitrator," served the game for forty years and set a record by umpiring eighteen World Series games. According to baseball historians Hy Turkin and S. C. Thompson, he also "started the practice of 'getting on the ball' by crouching to judge each pitch from right over the catcher's shoulders." (Charles Rigler was the first umpire to indicate a strike by jerking up his right thumb.) A famous Klem story involves the first time he ordered the obstreperous McGraw from a ball park:

"I'll have your job for this!" McGraw threatened.

"If that were possible," Klem replied, "then I don't want it."

Umpires came in all sizes, shapes and variety of temperaments. Klem, for example, was famous for drawing a line in the ground with his spikes; any argumentative player who crossed the line was automatically out of the game.

Big George Magerkurth, who weighed 230 pounds, once cleared the entire Brooklyn bench, leaving only the minimum number of players necessary to finish the game. Leo Durocher was thrown off the field before a game started, which did not set a precedent — it had happened to a manager before.

Willie Mays tells the story of how Whitey Lockman was once sent to the showers without opening his mouth because Umpire Driscoli "knew what you were fixing to say, and it's the same thing."

Long-range lenses on photographic cameras — and later, TV — complicated the labors of the men in blue, since the cameras could pinpoint glaring errors in judgment. Willie complained of two 500-foot homers taken away from McCovey as fouls "because the umpires didn't hustle the way they should have," but Willie had small reason to complain: more than once, balls he actually had trapped were called fair catches. So, in the end, the good breaks and the bad evened out, as every seasoned umpire and baseball player knew.

*　　*　　*　　*

It was easy for Willie to say what he pleased; his autobiography was published in 1966. Negroes by then had made their place in organized baseball, another reason why, quite aside from the fact that the St. Louis Cardinals had instigated regular Ladies Days in 1917, Branch Rickey deserved his place among the game's immortals. As Willie Mays well knew, Branch Rickey was the man who risked wrecking the National League for a principle.

As long ago as 1884, Moses Walker, a Negro and a graduate of Oberlin College, played major-league baseball for Toledo in the old American Association. Welday Walker, who was Moses' brother, also served Toledo as an utility outfielder, but Moses was the real pro: a good catcher with a season's batting average of .251. Louisville fans, among whom Southern prejudice ran high, made no secret of what would happen if Moses appeared in their park: they would lynch Moses at home plate.

Turned adrift into the minors, Moses joined the Newark, New Jersey team, where he became the battery mate of George Stovey, a Negro pitcher and 35-game winner in 1887. Newark was a classy club in those years and played exhibition games with the best teams in the majors, but Cap Anson refused to allow his Chicago White Stockings to take the field unless Stovey was benched.

Yet, Cap was not unique; racial dislike in those days amounted to hatred; and when Louis Sockalexis, the Penobscot Indian, played for

90

Cleveland, one of the numerous Delahanty clan* growled: "What's the league coming to, letting in them foreigners?" The reply, if any, that a full-blooded American Indian might have made to this comment has not been preserved. Perhaps that fact is just as well.

The nineteenth century saw other Negroes break into the minors — Clarence Matthews at short, Frank Grant at second, Charles Kelly at first, Bud Fowler at second — but none could hope to last long. An invisible wall existed between white man and black man, just as surely as though it had been constructed of concrete and steel. Among the early all-Negro teams that were organized was one called the Cuban Giants, who on the field even spoke a gibberish that sounded like Spanish, but they were Negroes recruited by a Frank Thompson from among fellow waiters in a hotel in Babylon, Long Island. (A half century ago, when I was a lad growing up in Brooklyn, the Cuban Giants were still well-known as a semi-pro team.)

Other all-Negro teams acquired respectable followings, and in 1920 a Negro National League was formed in Kansas City; the following year, a Negro Eastern League was organized, and in 1924, a Negro World Series was started. Smashed by the Great Depression of the early '30's, these two organizations finally were re-established as the Negro National and Negro American Leagues.

Great stars emerged among these Negro players. Experts who watched the curves and fast balls of Leroy (Satchel) Paige often wondered if this lanky, loose-jointed fellow was not the finest pitcher in baseball. "Old Satch," who came out of a poor Mobile, Alabama boyhood and pitched in any cow pasture where he could find an exhibition contest, has been called the only man to win 2,000 baseball games, and, just possibly, this claim may be true. Another story about "Old Satch" involved an exhibition game in Hawaii against one of the best pitchers in the major leagues; each bet the other $1,000 he would be the winner;

*Irish immigrants who settled in Cleveland, the Delahantys produced five sons who played in the majors — Ed, Frank, James, Joseph and Thomas — a family record. A sixth son, Willie, a star in the minors, was on his way to the majors when he was forced out of the game by being hit on the head by a pitch. Big Ed was the family's pride: in 1899, playing for Philadelphia, he hit .408 to lead the National League; then, in 1902, playing for Washington, his batting average of .376 led the American League. No player ever has duplicated this dual honor.

then each proceeded to pitch sixteen innings without yielding a hit — another tale that is completely believable.

Negro baseball produced other hurlers considered almost as good as "Old Satch" — Cyclone Joe Williams and Cannonball Dick Redding; there was, in addition, a celebrated Negro shortstop named John Henry Lloyd, a catcher named Josh Gibson, and an outfielder named Oscar Charleston who looked good enough to make any major-league team in the business.

And where there was no invisible line — in winter baseball played in Mexico, Cuba, Venezuela — Negroes frequently were the idols of the fans. How long American baseball might have clung to its wall of prejudice no one can say. It was willing to try, by all the evidence, when along came Branch Rickey.

And a remarkable young man named John Roosevelt Robinson.

Branch Rickey signs Jackie Robinson to a historic contract.

Good-By to Jim Crow

Molly Robinson was proud of her son Jackie: he was strong of body, bright of mind, brave of heart, and by nature a gentleman. She dreamed some day that he would be either a doctor or an athletic coach. He was a track star at Pasadena's Junior College, where he broke his brother Matthew's record in the broad jump, and later became an All-American halfback at University of California in Los Angeles.

Unlike Willie Mays, whose baseball-playing father started teaching him how to handle a baseball at the age of two, Jackie felt no inborn attraction toward the national pastime. Yet he played some baseball during the summer, first for a Pasadena team that became amateur champions of California, before he went off to serve in the army during the Second World War. He came home from that war a lieutenant, wanting to be married, yet even his fiancée thought he was wasting his time when he took a job as first baseman with the Kansas City Monarchs, a Negro team; but Jackie figured that the hundred bucks a week he received for playing was more dough than he could make from any other occupation.

Meanwhile, Branch Rickey had moved from boss of the St. Louis Cards to president of the Brooklyn Dodgers. Rickey intended to build a pennant-winner, which meant scouring the country for future baseball talent. "That might include a Negro player or two," Rickey told George V. McLaughlin, a banker of considerable influence in Dodgers affairs. A month later Rickey formed the United States League, a Negro organization, and one of its clubs was the Brooklyn Brown Dodgers.

The year was 1942, and Rickey, who must have been an insomniac for all the ideas racing through his mind, was dead serious in his intention to smash baseball's invisible line. Soon Clyde Sukeforth, the Dodgers coach, appeared in Kansas City. He watched the Monarchs, and mostly Jackie. This lad could hit. He ran bases like an antelope. Finally — and it took some doing — he convinced Jackie that far from being a crank he, Clyde Sukeforth, was telling the truth: the president of the Dodgers was most eager to see Jackie in Brooklyn.

The interview that followed between Branch Rickey and John Roosevelt Robinson was nothing if not historic; and for preserving its details, the baseball world owes a lasting debt to Arthur Mann for his excellent biography, *Branch Rickey, American in Action.* Jackie stared at an illuminated goldfish tank; Rickey puffed on a cigar. Jackie supposed he would be offered a place on some sort of colored team that was to play at Ebbets Field. Rickey, seated behind his massive walnut desk, blinked his bushy brows, perhaps waved aside a cloud of smoke, and put the matter straight:

"You were brought here, Jackie, to play for the Brooklyn organization. Perhaps on Montreal to start with ———"

Mann says that Jackie "gasped."

"Me? Play for Montreal?"

"If you can make it, yes," Rickey replied. "Later on — also if you can make it — you'll have a chance with the Brooklyn Dodgers."

The goldfish fluttered around the tank, but it is doubtful if Jackie saw them.

As a creative spirit, Branch Rickey was as big as his walnut desk, as big as the cigar he smoked. From his desk drawer he drew a copy of Papini's *Life of Christ,* a favorite book. He wanted Jackie to read it "as a guide to humility." One question recurred to Rickey. He asked it time and again:

"Can you take it? Can you take it?"

"They've been throwing at my head for a long time," Jackie said.

Rickey pictured a situation. The team was playing an important game. Jackie charged into second base and a collision occurred. The white second baseman called Jackie an unthinkable name. What then?

"Mr. Rickey," Jackie said, "do you want a ballplayer who's afraid to fight back?"

Rickey did. He paced the floor now. The hell with the fish in the tank, the cigar, the astonished Negro — Rickey knew what he wanted:

"You've got to do this job with base hits and stolen bases and fielding ground balls, Jackie. *Nothing else!"*

And Rickey asked some mean questions: How would Jackie

Roosevelt Stadium, Jersey City, N. J., April 18, 1946: Playing with the Montreal Royals against the Jersey City team, Jackie Robinson slides to safety during his first game in organized baseball.

respond to a pugnaciously loathsome hotel clerk in the South who refused him a room? Or to a sports writer who twisted his story to insult Jackie? Or if he were thrown out of dining rooms and railroad stations?

Rickey, a ham actor at heart, imagined Jackie in a World Series game. He hit Jackie "spikes first" at base. He jammed the ball into his ribs. A prejudiced umpire yipped, "You're out!" And Jackie, outraged, flared up, so they swung a fist at his face — and Rickey swung his own clenched hand, barely missing the target.

"What do you do?" Rickey demanded.

In a whisper, Jackie answered: "Mr. Rickey, I've got two cheeks. That it?"

That day John Roosevelt Robinson, who was willing to turn the other cheek, was hired by Branch Rickey.

*   *   *   *

Hector Racine of the Montreal club called a press conference on October 23, 1945, to announce the contractual signing of the first

Negro in professional baseball. A flurry of abuse from the smaller fry among sports writers should not have been unexpected; but the big-timers — notably Dan Parker of the now defunct *New York Mirror* — took "Robbie" in stride. Deep down in the South, in Greensboro, North Carolina, a sports writer for the *Daily News* wrote: "I don't see anything wrong with the signing of Jackie Robinson."

But not everyone in the South was either as mature or as tolerant as sports writer Smith Barrier: local authorities in one Florida town chased Jackie out for thinking he could appear on the same field with whites; a sheriff banned him from the bench in another southern town. Back in Kansas City, his old teammates on the Monarchs were predicting that Robinson would make a shambles out of the International League.

Jackie did not do that well. His hitting was off. In Baltimore, a few cries of "nigger" may have disconcerted him; in Syracuse, the riding was more disgraceful. But Jackie had courage. Running the base paths,

August 8, 1948: Jackie, a Brooklyn Dodger by then, is greeted at home plate after hitting a home run.

(Below) Jackie autographs baseballs, with manager Burt Shotten an interested bystander.

he had no equal. He stole second. He stole third. He stole home. And he drove pitchers off balance until they feared for their sanity.

But Jackie, tight though he might feel on the road, off stride, a man playing against himself, could always look forward to the home games in Montreal. Here the fans adored him, calling him, in their French accent, "Jah-*kee!*"

That year Montreal met Louisville in the Little World Series — Louisville, which in 1884 had threatened to lynch Moses Walker at home plate if he appeared on the field as the Toledo catcher. Kentucky hospitality fell apart; the sight of Jackie on the field wrote new terms of loathsomeness into the English language; and Jackie and the Montreal team suffered agonies, losing two games out of three.

For Jackie, at that moment, the fact that he would ever make the Dodgers must have seemed as far away as the moon — and as far away as Mars must have seemed the prospect that in 1947 he would be the National League's Rookie of the Year and in 1949 its Most Valuable Player.

But Montreal was waiting for Louisville, where the Little World Series would end. Nasty epithets the fans in Louisville may have invented; the Canadians could devise even wilder insults — especially when screeched in a combination of English and French — and again, my old friend, Robert Smith, in *Heroes of Baseball,* has captured in a single paragraph one of the unforgettable moments in organized baseball:

"Having batted only .200 while Montreal was dropping two out of three in Louisville*, Jackie walloped the ball for .400 in helping Montreal win the home three games. And when he scored the winning run in the game that meant the championship, the home fans almost tore down the park. The pitcher, the manager, and everyone got a ride around the park on the shoulders of the fans. But mostly they wanted Jah-kee, to whom they sang their own substitute for 'He's a Jolly Good Fellow,' the French song 'Il A Gagné ses Epaulettes.' They hugged Jackie, kissed him, pounded him, hoisting him high in the air while tears of happiness poured down his cheeks. Finally he begged off, got

---

*Actually, Jackie had led the International League that year, batting .349. He had stolen 40 bases.

into the clubhouse and hurried to dress for the plane that was to take him home. But when he opened the clubhouse door, he found the runway packed solid with more fans come to embrace him. He handed his suitcase to a friend and, after a few vain attempts to clear a way for himself, he put his shoulder down and bucked his way through, while men, women or kids reached out to caress him or slap his back. He found a clear opening at last, broke loose and started to run. Then the Canadian city saw its own version of a race riot — a Negro ball player running pell-mell down the middle of the street with five hundred screaming white fans on his heels, all bent on kissing him or wringing his hand. After Jackie had gone three blocks, while hundreds of people crowded out of homes and shops to join the mob, a man in a car stopped and gave Jackie a ride to his hotel. Jackie still gets a tight feeling in his chest when he recalls that day. 'That was the greatest thing that ever happened to me,' he says."

But it wasn't. Next season John Roosevelt Robinson went up to the Dodgers as a regular, which may have been not only the greatest thing that happened to Jackie, but also to a great many other Americans.

*   *   *   *

A strange situation began to develop in the National League that season, resulting in the suspension for a year of Leo Durocher, manager of the Brooklyn Dodgers. For a long time Happy Chandler, the Commissioner of Baseball, had been unhappy over stories about Leo the Lip: the fact that Durocher had spent a winter at the home of George Raft, "a movie actor long known for his suave and realistic portrayal of gangsters"; the fact that Leo knew certain underworld characters; the fact that John Christian, a Dodger fan who made comments Durocher did not like, had his jaw broken (the Dodgers settled a civil suit with Christian for $6,500); the fact that Leo's marriage to Laraine Day violated a California decree that she not remarry for a year and resulted in a contempt citation; the fact that Leo accused Larry McPhail of entertaining a well-known race handicapper and snapped at newspapermen: "Are there two sets of rules? One applying to managers and one to club owners?" McPhail, as the Yankee boss, branded Leo a liar and charged him with "conduct detrimental to baseball";

Photo sequence from a Dodger-Giant game that took place in September, 1954. Giant relief pitcher Hoyt Wilhelm, right center, breaks from pitching mound for roller hit by Dodger catcher Roy Campanella. Wilhelm is still trying, but unsuccessfully, to pick up the ball as Jackie Robinson romps home from third. Campanella made first safely. Catcher is Ray Catt (8), umpire is Al Barlick. In background, left, is Giant third baseman Hank Thompson. The Dodgers won the game, 7 to 4.

Chandler held two meetings and suspended Durocher. In Brooklyn, reliable Burt Shotton moved up to the managerial post.

At the height of the furore between McPhail and Durocher, Branch Rickey moved Jackie Robinson to the Dodgers.

A new tempest swept baseball.

McPhail was quoted as saying, "Serve the Negro in baseball best by letting the Negro leagues carry on in their own fashion." Jackie had good reason for re-reading Papini's *Life of Christ* and remembering Rickey's admonition about turning the other cheek.

The opposition Jackie experienced was tough, nasty, almost unbelievable. In Philadelphia, screams of "dirty nigger" sounded from the dugout.

Jackie was spiked. He was hipped hard. Balls were thrown at his head.

No one who then played on the Dodgers will admit today that he had threatened to quit the team if Robbie stayed, but at least one did. Here, there, an umpire deliberately picked a quarrel — umpires are not perfect.

From day to day the rumor grew more widespread: players throughout the league were going to strike unless the Dodgers dropped Robinson. Ford Frick, president of the National League, never lacked for backbone. His statement to his rebellious players deserves a place among the most forthright documents upon which American freedom rests:

"If you do this, you will be suspended from the league. . . . I do not care if half the league strikes. Those who do it will encounter quick retribution. All will be suspended and I don't care if it wrecks the National League. This is the United States of America and one citizen has as much right to play as another."

Under Frick's strong, courageous stand the so-called players' strike collapsed. Baseball at long last had said good-by to Jim Crow. Kind old Burt Shotton understood what Jackie was suffering: he was tense, awkward, not hitting well, convinced that he was doing ten times worse than was actually so.

But Burt could wait. He set Eddie Stanky to coaching Jackie in how to move around the base path for various hitters. Slowly Jackie

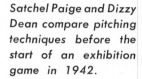

Roy Campanella, Dodger catcher, flips away his mask as he prepares to catch a ball fouled-off by batter.

Satchel Paige and Dizzy Dean compare pitching techniques before the start of an exhibition game in 1942.

improved and gained new confidence, until all at once Jackie was back in stride. On the base path he was phenomenal — stealing second, stealing third, even stealing home. He learned to take the hard knocks with a shrug, and the fans in Brooklyn, like the fans a season ago in Montreal, came to idolize him. Pitchers hated to have Jackie on base — sooner or later, hopping up and down the base path, he trapped them into a balk. His hitting, too, grew better. The Dodgers won the pennant that year — the same year, incidentally, when Cookie Lavagetto's double spoiled Bevens' no-hit World Series effort — but then, the Yankees were winning their fifth pennant, their fifth World Series championship, a story in itself.

Jackie — with assists from Branch Rickey and Ford Frick — had done what others had considered impossible: he had made baseball an All-American game. Roy Campanella, a Negro catcher (and one of the best), would join the Dodgers the following season. And in 1948, old Satchel Paige, then well past 40 years of age (and perhaps well past 60, for all anyone knew), joined the Cleveland team and helped to pitch the Indians into a pennant. And along came a great many other Negro stars into the majors: Larry Doby, Don Newcombe and Luke Easter, to name only a few, before one day appeared a player who may have been baseball's greatest luminary since Babe Ruth. His name was Willie Mays.

All Were Very Remarkable Men

Besides standing behind Branch Rickey with courage and intelligence in opening organized baseball to the Negro, Ford Frick's administration faced with equal realism the necessity of bolstering Philadelphia and Boston as the weakest clubs in the National League. Up in Beantown the miracle was achieved by Lou Perini, Guido Rugo and Joseph Maney — called the "Three Little Steam Shovels," because all had made their money from the construction business — and all were now willing to pour their money (as though it were cement) into making the Braves a pennant contender. They paid $40,000 for shortstop Alvin Dark, fresh out of Louisiana State University. They bought Eddie Stanky from the Dodgers. And along with Pitcher Johnny Sain, a right-hander, they had Warren Spahn, a southpaw. These two hurlers were really the sum of the Beantown mound staff, so that a popular jingle in Boston became: "Spahn, Sain, then pray for rain."

A story is told of how Casey Stengel, then managing the Boston Braves, fired Spahn in his rookie year. The Ol' Case was not perfect; and neither are the stories told about him. But this yarn has Stengel telling Spahn to go out and "dust off" a batter, which young Spahn could not conscientiously do; so, according to the tale, a furious Casey turned a torrent of abuse upon his rookie: "Young man, you're through with this team. Pick up your railroad ticket to go back to the minors. You've got no guts!"

The sentence sounds far too articulate for Stengel — he never expressed his remarks as simply as this, and one of the profoundest mistakes of the Office of Commissioner of Baseball was the fact that it never issued a "Dictionary of Stengelese" so that the rest of the world could know about what Case was talking. Spahn then was only twenty-one years of age; Ol' Case, born July 30, 1890, at Kansas City, had broken into the majors with Brooklyn in 1912. When Stengel sent the rookie back to the minors, it was the time of the Second World War, and Warren Spahn, far from lacking "guts," quit baseball to join the army.

Three years later Spahn returned with a presidential citation for bravery under fire. His baseball "jitters," spotted by Stengel, remained; but slowly, he recovered his stride, his confidence (among a Jackie Robinson, first Negro in baseball, a Warren Spahn, or any kid growing up, there is small distinction: all have the right to fail and then to succeed). And once Warren Spahn decided that he could pitch, he would become "the greatest southpaw pitcher of all time."

Pitching more innings than any left-hander in the business, Spahn won more games, struck out more hitters, accumulated more shutouts, and had more seasons of twenty victories or more than anyone in his time. At the age of forty-three, still pitching in the majors, Spahn had won better than 350 games. The one-time rookie, who then was playing for the Milwaukee Braves (where eventually the Boston franchise was

The southpaw pitching style of Warren Spahn, a consistent 20-game winner each season for the Milwaukee Braves, is clearly displayed in this photo sequence.

transferred), was earning $85,000 a year. By 1964 he would become the first pitcher in history who, over his lifetime, had earned more than a million dollars for throwing baseballs at opposing batters. And he possessed no greater admirer — if you could *un*-mix the words to understand this fact — than Casey Stengel.

*   *   *   *

Of Warren Spahn, Willie Mays, the hero of our next chapter, once said: "Many people think I've taken care of Spahnie over the years. He's taken care of me, too. And when I say 'take care,' I don't mean 'protect.' I mean, I hit him, or he strikes me out. The ledger's been a long one, and a pretty even one, between us."

But fortunately for Spahn, the number-one hitter in his best years was not Willie Mays, but Ted Williams of the Boston Red Sox, who came up to the majors in 1939, hitting .327. Ted, then nicknamed "The Kid," was twenty-one years old; and everyone began to wonder if this son of San Diego, California might not some day equal the record of Hugh Duffy who, playing for Boston in 1894, hit a respectable .438. In Ted's third year in the majors, 1941, he rapped out .406, and all of Boston realized that, since the days of Duffy, old Beantown never had possessed such a slugger.

Batting averages were falling, not rising, when Ted slammed out his .406 in 1941, a fact that drew attention to his performance. Only sixteen batters in the American League had hit over .300 that season, another factor which made the experts lift their eyebrows. Sure, George Sisler, the "Gorgeous," playing for St. Louis in 1922, had hit .420, but thirty-three American League players had batted over .300 that season, and baseball is full of nuts who keep statistics like these. If Ted Williams could have had his name and record placed into a modern computer, when the wheels stopped spinning, a single word would issue from the machine: "Stupendous!"

In 1941, Williams, a stringbean weighing somewhere around 175 pounds as compared to the 200 pounds of "muscular heft" of "burly Jimmy Foxx," possessed a smooth, perfect timing that gave him prodigious power at bat.

"That swing," wrote Dwight Freeburg in the magazine *Baseball,*

(Above) Ted Williams, a formidable left-handed batter and "long-ball" hitter, is at the plate in the first game of the 1946 World Series at Sportsman's Park, bringing on the tactically defensive "Ted Williams shift" by the opposing St. Louis Cardinals' infield. Marty Marion remains at shortstop, but third baseman Whitey Kurowski shifts to normal second-base place and second baseman Red Schoendienst moves over closer to Stan Musial at first. (Right) Ted connects for another long one in a 1957 game against the Chicago White Sox. Catcher is Sherm Lollar.

Three generations of baseball Sislers are shown in this picture which was taken in 1953: (left to right) George Sisler, Jr., General Manager of the Red Birds; George Sisler, Sr., head of the Pittsburgh Pirates' scouting system at the time and member of Baseball's Hall of Fame; and Dick Sisler, George Jr.'s son, a Columbus outfielder.

105

"is so perfect that even a hitter like Joe DiMaggio admits that he studies it." Williams, who had stood for hours in front of a mirror studying his own swing, fascinated Freeburg.

"He led his nearest competitor, the splendid hitter [Cecil] Travis of Washington, by 47 batting points. He led the great Joe DiMaggio by 49. And when you beat anyone by nearly fifty points, actual competition ceases." Freeburg was willing to go further, proving that in long-distance hitting (called "slugging percentage" by the experts), Ted had led DiMaggio by 91 points and Travis by 215.* Going completely scientific, Freeburg went back two decades to when the sacrifice-fly rule "did not add a time at bat" and concluded that only two hitters, Sisler and Rogers Hornsby,** could have joined Ted's class. Ty Cobb, hitting .420, .410 and .401, would have had two of these seasons thrown out under Freeburg's rule, although, quieting down somewhat, Freeburg was willing to confess that Ted's "slashing bat" had not yet made him the equal of "the fiery Ty" or "the famous Babe."

But Freeburg was right in his hunches: earlier than most he marked Ted Williams for greatness, who, after the Second World War, would smack out consecutive averages of .342, .343, .369, .342. In giving advice to youngsters, Ty Cobb once said: "The best hitters stand up and have the look of a good hitter." Ted Williams did. And in the decade after the Second World War, he may have been the greatest of all sluggers, but baseball is a big game, and even Ted Williams had to share headlines.

*   *   *   *

For example, there was Stan (The Man) Musial, whose real middle name was Frank. Born November 21, 1920, of immigrant parents (Polish on his father's side, Czech on his mother's side), Stan greeted the world in the dismal town of Donora, Pennsylvania. In this drab steel-and-coal country of western Pennsylvania, Stan's family earned a living by sorting nails in a lumber mill, and his childhood was

---

*Actually, DiMaggio collected 13 more total bases than Williams that season. This was the year when DiMaggio hit in 56 consecutive games.

**The Texas-born Hornsby hit .401 in 1922, .424 in 1924, .403 in 1925, .400 in 1936.

scrimpy, hard and probably half-hungry. It was the kind of environment whence by any means, at any age, a sane human being would escape: Stan, marrying his childhood sweetheart, Lillian Labash, at the age of nineteen, chose a career in baseball and fled.

That in time (despite Jackie Robinson) Stan would become the most spectacular star produced by Branch Rickey, who then managed the St. Louis Cardinals, was of small meaning to Musial — he was rid of Donora. He began life as a left-handed pitcher with Williamson in the Mountain States League, thanks largely to the efforts of Andy French, a Cardinal scout who had watched Stan playing with his home-town high school team. Williamson was better than Donora: there was no steel-mill smog here; and there was even less smog in Daytona Beach in the Florida State League, where Stan played in 1940 and won 18 games and lost 5.

On off days, because of Stan's hitting, he was employed in the outfield. Injured while making a diving catch at a ball in a game against Orlando one August day in 1940, Stan's pitching days ended. His wife then was expecting a baby, and Stan, earning only $100 a month six months in the year, believed his baseball career also had ended. The manager at Daytona Beach was Dickie Kerr, who had emerged an honest man from the Chicago Black Sox scandal of 1919; he gave the Musials a home and they named their baby Richard, in Kerr's honor.

When Stan went to the mass training camp at Columbus, Georgia, that the Cardinals held for minor-league players in the spring of 1941, he must have held small hope for success. The Cardinals, after all, were one of the roughest, toughest teams in baseball — producers of the "Gashouse Gang" that included players like Joe Medwick and Leo Durocher, and pitchers like Dizzy Dean, one of the immortals, who one day said his first name was Jerome and the next that it was Jay, and who in one breath claimed Arkansas as his birthplace and in the next said he had been born in Oklahoma.

But under Branch Rickey, some of this wackiness had been toned down; and Burt Shotton, who would nurse Jackie Robinson through his first season in the majors, then managed the Cards. Burt was not too worried over Stan's injured left arm, which made him a poor pitching prospect; Burt, whose extremely sensitive baseball nose sniffed the

107

Stan "The Man" Musial in 1946. Shown are (left) his batting stance; (upper center) his keen eyes; (lower center) his grip on the bat; and (right) his spontaneous grin.

scent of a potential great outfielder, sent Stan for seasoning with Springfield in the Western Association. Stan played a half-season with Springfield and hit .379, then moved up to Rochester in the International League where he played 54 games and hit .326; and so, in September, Burt brought him back to play the last twelve games of the season with the Cards. Stan belted National League pitching for a .426 average in those last twelve games.

Lee Allen, who wrote the official history of the National League, understood why the son of Donora's smog became a baseball tradition:

"A left-handed hitter who keeps his feet close together, Musial looks at the pitcher over his right shoulder, springing out of a crouch to hit the ball. As the years passed, the crouch became more pronounced, and when he came out of the Navy to rejoin his team in 1946, his style, though natural, was too extreme to be imitated. It was Ted

Lyons, the veteran White Sox pitcher, who first described Stan's batting style as that of a 'kid peeking around the corner to see if the cops were coming.' "

The "kid" frequently hit and ran before the "cop" on the mound knew he was there. At the end of the 1960 season, Lee Allen not only had decided that Stan was "one of the greatest players in National League history," but suggested some convincing statistics in behalf of his conclusion:

Category	Musial's Total	Rank
Games played	2644	Fourth
Times at bat	9830	Third
Runs	1812	Second
Hits	3294	Second
Singles	2020	Tenth
Doubles	675	First
Triples	170	Tenth
Home Runs	429	Second
Total Bases	5596	First
Runs-batted-in	1741	Second
Batting Percentage	.335	Eleventh
Slugging Percentage	.569	Fourth

The fans always wanted Stan to make records that no one could tie. These objectives he never achieved, but as "Stan the Man," the son of Donora, Pennsylvania, he stands by himself.

* * * *

When the suspension was lifted on "Leo the Lip" Durocher, he came back to the National League so quietly that he was called "Leo the Little Shepherd." The Giants, needing a manager to replace Mel Ott, decided midway in July of 1948 on Leo. The result was devastating. Giant fans who for years had hated Leo as the old Dodgers manager were now supposed to fall in love with him, and more surprisingly, they did so, as Leo raised the Giants higher in the National League standings, season after season.

National League baseball was going through a cycle of mysterious events. The Dodgers, battling the Phillies in the tenth inning of the last game in 1949, won the pennant in a season when Ralph Kiner had hit 54 home runs for Pittsburgh: it was a crazy year. A Philadelphia first baseman, Eddie Waitkus, was shot by a girl in a Chicago hotel who believed he would never return her secret love for him. Happily, Waitkus recovered and rejoined the Phillies who, known as "the Whiz Kids," went on to win the pennant by two games over the Dodgers.

The Giants, under Leo the Silent Lip, finished fifth in 1949. Durocher, who was never a fool, knew exactly how to rebuild his team. He bought shortstop Alvin Dark and second baseman Eddie Stanky from the Boston Braves, a brilliant deal that gave him at long last a double-play combination. By 1950, with Dark and Stanky, the Giants finished third and Leo the Lip grew more articulate. In Larry Jensen and Sal Maglie the Giants acquired two exceptional pitchers; then Jim Hearn, bought from the Cardinals, gave Leo the leverage he needed to scale the heights. Raw statistics tell the story of 1951: on August 11, Leo's Giants were 13½ games behind the Dodgers; Leo, driving his club to win 16 games in a row, was still 6 games behind, but the Lip kept talking, kept driving, and on the last day of the season the Giants tied for the pennant.

Old Dodger fans (I among them) hate the rest of this story. The first play-off game, with Jim Hearn pitching against Ralph Branca, was won at Ebbets Field by the Giants, 3 to 1. Up at the Polo Grounds, the Dodgers looked deep into their bullpen and picked Clem Labine, not much of a pitcher, but good enough that day to knock off the Giants, 10 to 0. They danced all over Brooklyn that night; and then, sobering up, faced a duel between Sal Maglie for the Giants and Don Newcombe for the Dodgers that could go either way.

The Dodgers went into the ninth inning leading 4 to 1. But no Dodger fan could ever forget what had happened in the World Series of 1941 when catcher Mickey Owen allowed a third strike to slip through his glove. The Yankee runner reached first and the Dodgers broke wide open. Heinrich raced safely to first base and the Yankees went on to win the game 7 to 4 (and the Series, 4 games to 1).

Now, leading in the 1951 playoff — but remembering Mickey Owen — Dodger fans were worried. And they had reason to be.

The date was October 3, 1951 — to Willie Mays, "the most famous single date . . . in baseball history." The Giants had come up

110

to the end of the season winning 38 out of their last 46 games, 13 out of their last 15, and yet all this effort was wasted, *unless* —

Don Newcombe, a Negro pitcher for the Dodgers, was one of the greatest in the trade, but Leo the Lip was not overawed. "We've still got a chance to win," he said, more profanely than these words suggest.

Alvin Dark, first up for the Giants, singled between Gil Hodges at first and Jackie Robinson at second, causing both infielders, in Willie's words, to cross themselves "like the blades of a scissors coming together." Don Mueller, following Dark, hit almost the same kind of ball. Don Newcombe wiped a hand across his big, black sweaty face; two on, no out, the situation was dangerous: most of all with Monte Irvin, a power hitter, striding to the plate. Irvin fouled out. Up to the plate came Whitey Lockman — he wrote "Lock" on one shoe and "Man" on the other, so that unless they spelled his name when placed side by side, he knew one had been stolen; Lockman's double scored Dark. Mueller, sliding into third, sprained his ankle; and Floppy Hartung was sent to run for him.

Out of the Dodgers dugout came manager Charley Dressen, wearing a scowl that reached to his heels. In the batter's circle waited Willie Mays, but Willie was not yet the magic boy of the National League; on Charley's mind was the presence in the batter's box of that canny Scot, Bobby Thomson, who, over the course of the season, had hit two home runs off Carl Erskine and one each off the offerings of Preacher Roe, Newcombe and Phil Haugstad.

So Dressen had reason to fear Thomson as he called Ralph Branca from the bullpen and waited as Newcombe politely handed the ball to Branca, shook hands, and walked off the field with a bleeding heart. Two days before, Bobby Thomson had hit a home run off Ralph Branca in the first game of the play-off; Dressen had to make the difficult decision: pitch to Thomson or walk him? Charley decided to pitch.

Dressen simply could not go against the hoariest strategy in baseball — he could not purposely put the winning run on base. Two runs ahead, thought Charley. Heck, pitch to Thomson, Charley decided. Branca threw a strike, a fast ball that cut the middle of the plate. Overwhelmed by his success, Branca tried the fast ball again

"The shot heard round the (baseball) world." (Right) Bobby Thomson of the Giants belts the home run that won the play-offs and the National League pennant, October 3, 1951. (Far right) Andy Pafko of the Dodgers watches helplessly as Thomson's ball sails into the Polo Grounds' left field stands.

and the game was over, for the canny Scot, waiting patiently, expecting the pitch, tagged it. No one doubted where the ball was going — into the left field stands.

And so the game was over and New York would never forget its Cinderella team, nor would anyone in Brooklyn. And few tears were shed in Brooklyn when the Giants, winning the first game of the World Series, went on to lose the championship in six games. The bat that Thomson used to hit his home run is in the Hall of Fame at Cooperstown. No true, old-time Dodger fan — like myself — ever wishes to look at it.

*   *   *   *

After 1936, with Joe McCarthy managing the club, the New York Yankees were the team that everyone wanted to break up. Their pennant-winning record was incredible: 1936 (won 102, lost 51, percentage .667); 1937 (won 102, lost 52, percentage .662); 1938 (won 99, lost 53, percentage .651); 1939 (won 106, lost 45, percentage .702); 1941 (won 101, lost 53, percentage .656); 1942 (won 103, lost 51, percentage .669); 1943 (won 98, lost 56, percentage .636); 1947 (won 97, lost 57, percentage .630);* 1949 (won 97, lost 57, percentage .630);* 1950 (won 98, lost 56, percentage .636).

*Bucky Harris managed the team in 1947; Casey Stengel in 1949 and 1950.

Nor was the World Series record of the New York Yankees less impressive during these years: in 1937, they turned back the Giants, 4 games to 1; in 1938, the Chicago Cubs, 4 games to 0; in 1939, Cincinnati, 4 games to 0; in 1941, the Brooklyn Dodgers, 4 games to 1; in 1942, they lost to the St. Louis Cards, 4 games to 1, a result that they reversed in 1943; in 1947, they beat the Brooklyn Dodgers, 4 games to 3; in 1949, they walloped the Dodgers again, 4 games to 1; in 1950, they overwhelmed the Philadelphia "Whiz Kids," 4 games to 0.

An earlier play in the fifth inning saw hero-to-be Bobby Thomson making a successful dive for second base as he completed his double down the left field line. Awaiting Andy Pafko's throw from left field is Dodger second baseman Jackie Robinson . . .

. . . who catches the ball and turns toward the sack. But Thomson is there, too, arriving in a full-length slide . . .

. . . and is called safe by umpire Bill Stewart as Robinson flops over.

Many players helped the Yankees climb to this phenomenal success, but only one would capture the public's affection almost as irresistibly as the Babe. Known in time as "the Yankee Clipper," Joseph Paul DiMaggio was one of three baseball players born to an Italian fisherman in San Francisco. Vince and Dom were good baseball men; Joe was an "immortal" almost from the moment he began knocking a ball around the neighborhood playground in Golden Gate Park.

Yet it was Vince who got Joe his start playing in organized baseball, and by the spring of 1934, Joe was the most talked-about outfielder in the Pacific Coast League. The season before — 1933 — Joe had hit in 61 consecutive games for the San Francisco Seals; his average was .340. And Joe simply grew better from season to season; the Seals, in no hurry to drop this barrel of dough into the majors, were willing to wait for the right price. The price tag on Joe kept going up — to $60,000, to $75,000.

But in this process of bargaining, scouting reports took on a critical note. How about Joe's left leg when he ran? Didn't it drag somewhat?

The tactics of baseball as a big business never worked more perfectly — Joe was haggled over as though he were a broken-down gun on a battlefield who might possibly be of some use in a pinch — and so, ultimately, in what Frank Graham has called "the greatest buy in the history of modern baseball," Joe went to the New York Yankees for $25,000. In 1935, his last season with the Seals, the future "Great DiMag" hit .398. In the front office, Yankee officials rubbed together their hands and chuckled: Joe's 270 hits that year had included 48 doubles, 18 triples, 34 home runs.

DiMaggio's batting averages with New York, beginning in 1936, fell under .300 only once (1946). The following year he was back to .315, and kept climbing while "the Yankee Clipper" was called "Joltin' Joe" when the headline writers needed a switch, until he was smashing records as a matter of habit.

In 1897, Wee Willie Keeler thrilled the Red Sox by hitting in 44 consecutive games, but Joe cracked that mark in 1941 by going through 56 games with 91 hits in 223 times at bat, for an average

Vince DiMaggio

during this hitting streak of .408 (he scored 56 runs, drove in 55 and racked up 15 homers).

That season the Yankees won the pennant from the Red Sox by 17 games and came up against the Dodgers who, after 21 years, finally had won the National League flag. The year was the one when Mickey Owen dropped his famous third strike and the Yankees won the championship, 4 games to 1.

Joseph Paul DiMaggio, son of an Italian fisherman — Warren Spahn, fired by Casey Stengel for refusing to dust off a batter — Ted Williams, "The Kid" who made good — Stan Musial, who "pounced" on the ball — Leo the Lip coming back as Leo the Little Shepherd — Bobby Thomson, the Scot who broke a million hearts in Brooklyn . . . such were some of the ingredients that made baseball a bigger national pastime after the Second World War. And it would grow even bigger. One of the reasons why was a hitter who, heart in throat, waited in the on-batter's circle, knowing the destiny of the Giants would rest on his shoulders unless Bobby Thomson outguessed Ralph Branca's pitching. He was a Negro player — the son of "Kitty-Kat" Mays.

(Below) Joe DiMaggio came up to bat in his first formal appearance with the New York Yankees on April 30, 1938 (in Washington, D. C.) and promptly whammed out a high fly for a single. Watching the flight as the ball leaves Joe's bat in this picture is Joe, himself, and catcher Rick Ferrell of the Washington Senators.

Joe DiMaggio receives the 1947 Most Valuable Player Award for the American League on April 23, 1948. Pictured left to right are: Baseball Commissioner A. B. "Happy" Chandler; Joe DiMaggio; Joe King (President of the Baseball Writers Association); and Governor Thomas E. Dewey.

115

Kitty-Kat's Kid and Other Characters

Willie Mays (in an excellent autobiography written with Charles Einstein) tells how his first ambition was to be a cowboy. His father, whose real name was William Howard Mays (he was born when William Howard Taft was President), changed Willie's direction very early in life. Willie was born May 6, 1931, in the Alabama town of Westfield. Before a year had ended, the marriage of his father and mother broke up, and so Willie went to live with his Aunt Sarah in nearby Fairfield. "They were kids themselves, my mother and father — no more than 18, either one of them," Willie said. There would never be an ounce of bitterness in Willie. His mother was a track star, his father a baseball player — the two strains mixed well.

Willie was less than two years old when his father, whose nickname was "Kitty-Kat," started the lad to catching a baseball. He taught him that sneaky catch for which Willie is famous — that running pick-up which to this day umpires can not tell whether the ball is taken on a bounce or fly (and Willie is not going to tell them). By day Willie's dad worked in a Birmingham steel mill, a rotten job; weekends he played with the Birmingham Barons, a good semipro team. In later years, when Willie had become perhaps the greatest baseball player this generation would produce, a scout told him of the man he might never equal:

"Your old man. Kitty-Kat. Lots of things you can do, he couldn't do. But *graceful?* Man, he was a poem. He was Shakespeare and that other cat Dante rolled into one. Know the difference, Buck [Willie's early nickname was 'Buckhand']? You don't *pounce.* You're a grabber. The old man, though — that's why we called him Kitty-Kat — now, *he* knew how to *pounce!*" It must have been a beautiful sight to see.

Kitty-Kat was sure of one thing: his son Willie was not going to waste his life sweating away in a Birmingham steel mill. At school he took a course in cleaning and pressing — anything extra he earned on the side was all to the good. But Willie was playing with the Barons while still a teen-ager. In a factory game came a moment when father and son faced a crisis. But let Willie tell the story:

". . . In the second inning, one of the hitters, a left-handed batter, looped a long, sinking liner to left-center, the wrong field for him, and I heard my father say, 'All right, all right, let me take it!' But then I was aware that the ball was sinking and he was too far back, and I knew if I cut in front of him I could handle it, and caught it off the grass-tops.

"And I knew also that I had shown him up.

"And he knew it.

"I've never apologized to him for making the play.

"He's never apologized to me for trying to call me off.

"We both wanted the same thing — to get away from the situation where I had to play side by side in the same outfield with my own father."

In 1963, before the first encounter of the year in New York between the San Francisco Giants and the New York Mets, the fans held pre-game ceremonies honoring Willie Mays. There was room in their hearts for both the new home team and for Willie, who was not forgotten as "their" boy when the Giants were the local team at the Polo Grounds.

Willie Mays is an acknowledged wizard on the base path, but he can't always make it home. Here he is tagged by catcher Del Wilber of the Philadelphia Phillies as he backslides in his attempt to score.

Kitty-Kat loved the kid, knew what he had produced in the way of a baseball player, and placidly waited for Willie to reap the rewards. The scout who watched Willie playing with the Birmingham Black Barons confidently told the Giant organization that he would be playing in the Polo Grounds within two years. Willie, who one day would become the highest-paid player in baseball, was offered $5,000, and when Willie signed with the Giant organization, Kitty-Kat "was a proud man." Willie, said Eddie Montague, possessed "a great arm." Watching him at batting and fielding practice, Montague added, "my eyes almost popped out of my head"; he saw a young colored boy who could "swing the bat with great speed and power, and with the quickness of a young Joe Louis throwing punches." Said Montague, unabashedly: "This was the greatest young ball player I had ever seen in my life or my scouting career."

Willie had just turned 19 when in 1950 he played with Trenton, New Jersey, a Giant farm team in the Interstate League. He played in 81 games, batted .353, drove in 55 runs and collected four homers.

Next Willie went to Minneapolis, where, he said, the "fans took me to their hearts," as well they should have: Willie hit .477 and his slugging average (calculated on total bases divided by times at bat) was .799. One of Willie's line drives put a hole in the fence of Bochert Field in Milwaukee. The beer barons still talk about that hole.

On May 25, 1951, Willie was called up to the New York Giants and distinguished himself by going to bat twelve times without a hit. The Giants won all these games, perhaps accounting for Leo Durocher's good humor over Willie's jittery slump. Finally, against Warren Spahn, Willie got his first major-league hit — a home run — and the Giants lost the game, 4 to 1. But that's baseball. Willie would have other slumps — Willie, who today is second to Babe Ruth in driving the most home runs — and just possibly, if Willie's legs hold up over enough seasons, Kitty-Kat's kid may set a new record.

But Willie is no fool: he can tell you about the speed of pitches — Walter Johnson of the Senators was said to be able to throw a ball at 117 miles per hour, though it was never measured. A throw by Cleveland's Bob Feller (the first to be measured) was clocked by the U. S. Army at 98.6 miles per hour. Willie did not care too much about such tales. A real pitcher — say, a Sandy Koufax, a Robin Roberts, a Don Newcombe — was not going to leave a batter alone when the count went to 0-2. That next pitch, more than likely, was going to be in, and if a Willie Mays watched it sail by, Willie was out on strikes.

What makes a legend out of a Willie Mays, a Babe Ruth? The games they play, the home runs they hit, the salaries they demand? Or could it be moments like these, recounted in the words of Kitty-Kat's kid:

"My own hospital visits take place as much out of season as in. Maybe even more so, because people know there's no baseball schedule to get in the way, so the number of requests becomes greater. And this may work out the right way, because the reason they want you there is that the kids look up to you, and the reason the kids look up to you is that you do well at baseball, and one of the ways to make sure you do well at baseball is not to be sad and down and depressed in your mind, and when you have come away from a hospital room where the kid was in a coma and you were the first person he recognized or spoke to since the accident, and when his parents and nurses broke down and cried in the room because of what happened — and because they knew only a miracle would ever make the kid well again, or even keep him from dying — then you have seen this with your own eyes, and you know that they think you were this miracle — or you know they knew you weren't, but still the kid was happy to see you. Sometimes, afterward by yourself, you cry some, too."

Willie could remember faces, but not names. On meeting a person for the second time, to cover his embarrassment, he would shout, "Say, Hey!" — and so he became known as the Say-Hey Kid. But he will be remembered in history as Kitty-Kat's kid, and within his own generation (give or take a decade) he will belong to a great stream of baseball immortals.

For an example, take Casey Stengel.

*   *   *   *

On July 4, 1890, Charles Dillon Stengel was born in a Kansas City hospital, and the fact that this Missouri city was known everywhere as "K.C.," may have explained why the lad would be called in later years "Casey" Stengel. Some authorities say that Stengel derived his nickname from "Casey at the Bat," but Casey was never this good as a hitter. An older brother, Grant, was a better player than Casey — in fact, Grant secured Casey's first job playing baseball. In his junior year, Casey pitched for his Central High School nine; that year, in fifteen innings, Casey hurled Central to a 7-6 victory over Joplin, perhaps the greatest triumph in his career. The Kansas City club, then a team in the American Association, decided that the best player in the state was Casey Stengel, who picked up a dollar wherever he could playing for such nines as the Parisian Cloak Company and Armour & Company.

Casey, at nineteen, was sent by Kansas City to Kankakee in the Northern Association. Throughout a long lifetime, one of Casey's favorite words was "nutsy" — and Casey was that, just a mite. At Kankakee, Casey used to fill in idle moments at center field practicing sliding into his own glove. The authorities shook their heads and predicted that "guys with butterfly nets are gonna come out here some day and bag him for that big place [the mental hospital] over there."

120

Before the boys with the butterfly nets caught up to Casey, he had gone on to Aurora in the Wisconsin-Illinois League, hit .352 and stolen 50 bases — he was the pride of the team. Bought by the Brooklyn Dodgers, he was sent to Montgomery in the Southern Association where, by luck, Casey fell in with Kid Elberfeld, who, as a shortstop, had been a veteran of the professional baseball hustings for fourteen years. The Kid, like tens of thousands who would come later, simply fell in love with Casey, his "nutsy" talk, his "nutsy" ways, his "nutsy" eagerness to learn. So Elberfeld took Casey in hand, teaching him all he knew about the game, and the Kid must have been a fine instructor, for Casey absorbed it all so well that to this day, some fifty years later, he can still spiel off (if given two or three hours) everything Elberfeld told him.

To accept Casey as the greatest baseball genius who may ever have inhabited this planet, one must take him at his own word. He is "nutsy." No one else in the game would tip his hat to the crowd and have a bird fly out. No one else, during a game, would hide in a sewer hole in center field and then pop out at the psychological moment to catch a fly. No one else would pack his trunk at three o'clock in the morning and then pace the floor until the hotel dining room opened for breakfast. No one else would cram a thousand words into a sentence, without punctuation, and make every bit of it sound fascinatingly lyrical, even though you, as the listener, might not comprehend a single word. No one else can recall plays half a century old — reconstructing them perfectly — or batting averages — or the names of saloons where he first met this veteran player or that — or what the numbers on the dice were when Bill Dahlen, managing the Dodgers when Casey moved up from Montgomery to Brooklyn, interrupted the clubhouse crap game by asking Stengel acidly: "You come up here to gamble or to play ball?"

Casey had come to play baseball — and to go on learning in his own "nutsy" manner: under hitters like Zack Wheat ("a wonderful hitter," in Casey's estimation, who smacked out "line drive after line drive"); and under managers like Bill Dahlen and Uncle Wilbert Robinson (so beloved in Brooklyn that for a time the Dodgers were called the Robins); and later, under managers like Gavvy Cravath and Wild Bill Donovan in Philadelphia, Hugo Bezdek in Pittsburgh, and that greatest of all managerial pepperpots, John J. McGraw of the New

York Giants. Uncle Wilbert Robinson was the greatest fun for Casey — he would argue anything from "huntin' dogs" to "corn likker"; Bezdek, who had coached football at Penn State, was the scholar, testing Casey's knowledge both of the history and the technique of the game (and perhaps accounting for why in years to come Casey himself also would be known as "The Perfessor"); but "the greatest manager," "the strictest," the one "who told you off in language you'd remember better than the others" was McGraw. Said Casey of McGraw:

"He always wanted every play executed properly, an' no alibis. If you couldn't execute after three or four tries, he'd decide that you were either too dumb or too awkward to play for him.

"Then he would trade you. But if you improved, he would probably get you back. He didn't stay stubbornly with his first opinion. He always traded you with the thought, 'I can buy this man back if he gets better an' he can help me win.'

"He made you make the big effort, made you put out all the time. He wanted you to fight the ball, not just stand there. He was good at startin' double steals, at seein' that his men ran the bases alertly. He was a wonderful manager, particularly offensively. And no manager adapted his game better from the dead ball we used to play to the lively ball we use today."*

Casey's six seasons with Brooklyn were not distinguished: his best batting average after playing 126 games in 1914 was .316; he was an in-and-outer with Pittsburgh and Philadelphia; and McGraw drew the best out of him (in 84 games in 1922 Casey hit .368; in 75 games the following season he hit .339). To begin with, Casey had thought of major-league baseball only as a means of paying his tuition through dental college; but he was a left-handed tooth-puller, which had certain disadvantages (especially in Casey's version of his first patient, "I forgot to lower the chair an' then pulled instead of twistin' first an' the fella come leapin' outa the chair"), so Casey decided to stick with baseball.

*   *   *   *

The Giants sold Casey to the Boston Braves where during the next two seasons Stengel realized that his playing days were nearing an end:

---

*Quoted from Mitchell, Jerry, *The Amazing Mets* (1964). If Casey ever talked as articulately as this, the result amounted to a baseball revolution.

in 1925, he participated in only twelve games and hit .077. But Casey, dreaming of a new career, moved that May to become manager and president of Worcester in the Eastern League; then, when a better offer came along to manage Toledo in the American Association and the owner of the Worcester club refused to release him, Casey wrote a famous letter to the Commissioner of Baseball:

"Manager Casey Stengel is hereby and as of this date dismissed as manager of the Worcester Eastern League club. Signed: Charles Dillon Stengel, President, Worcester Baseball Club."

Casey managed Toledo for six years and became a major-league manager for the first time in 1935, when he replaced Max Carey as pilot of the Dodgers. These were by far some of the worst years in Brooklyn's baseball history — indeed, its first-rate players could be counted on the fingers of one hand — and Bill Terry, then managing the Giants, asked reporters: "Is Brooklyn still in the league?" For this remark Terry earned the eternal enmity of Dodger fans (who, if they were honest, admitted in their hearts that the game their team played resembled comedy rather than top-flight baseball), and under Stengel the Dodgers finished sixth, fifth and seventh. Casey, relieved of his duties but paid his salary for 1937, spent most of that year seeking an oil well in Texas. His salary of $15,000 quickly disappeared and so, too, did his hope of reaping a fortune from the oil business. Anyhow, "nutsy" though the fact might seem, baseball was in his blood. So Casey went back to six years of managing the Boston Braves — "pretty lean" years, as one expert observed, when Casey called his players "road apples" — and a broken leg in 1943 took him out of baseball for another year.

The career of the greatest manager baseball may ever have produced looked ended; but Ol' Case (perhaps the secret of his genius) gathered friends like the early-day blossoms on a morning-glory vine — there was always someone willing to take just one more gamble on Stengel. And now The Perfessor's truly colossal knowledge of the game began to pay off: at Milwaukee, where he won the American Association pennant by seven games; at Oakland, where he finished second and then fourth and then first. Meanwhile, Joe McCarthy, who had raised the New York Yankees to world renown, had developed a

Master "needler" Casey Stengel, managing the Boston Braves at the time of this photo, demonstrates the delicate art of umpire baiting.

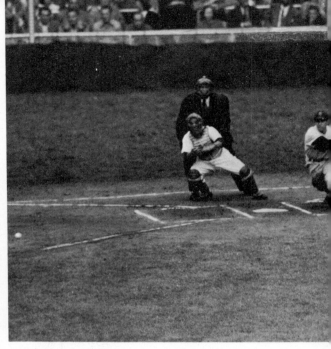

Scene from the first game of the 1949 World Series between the Dodgers and the Yankees: Allie Reynolds of the Yankees is the pitcher, Yogi Berra is the catcher, and Pee Wee Reese is the Brooklyn Dodgers' lead-off hitter. (Yankee first baseman Tommy Henrich made an unassisted putout at first.)

chronic stomach disorder. Suppose Joe had to go? No friend loved Ol' Case better than George Weiss, in charge of the Yankee farm system; Weiss declared he knew just the man to take McCarthy's place.

When Weiss mentioned Stengel, the Yankee general manager, Ed Barrow, reputedly all but blew his lid:

"That clown!"

Weiss talked persuasively, swearing that Casey was so devoted to baseball, "it pours out of him." True, "The Perfessor" might do things that would surprise Barrow, like sending up left-handed pinch-hitters against left-handed pitchers, but, Weiss suggested softly, why did not Barrow look up the scouting reports on Casey's managerial record at Oakland? Barrow surrendered, mayhap secretly agreeing with the *Bos-*

1

Casey Stengel, manager of the year, receives enthusiastic congratulations from Yankee owners Dan Topping (left) and Del Webb (right) in a dressing room celebration after the Yankees won the 1949 World Series.

ton Record that "the Yankees have now been mathematically eliminated from the 1949 pennant race" (which may have been justifiable bragging, since the season before, the Yankees had finished third behind Cleveland and Boston).

Casey stepped noisily into his new role, winning, for a starter, the 1949 pennant and World Series. "The Perfessor" knew that he was no longer managing "road apples," but one of the greatest collections of baseball talent ever assembled: Charley "King Kong" Keller, George "Snuffy" Stirnweiss, Joe DiMaggio, Phil Rizzuto, Yogi Berra, Mickey Mantle, Johnny Lindell, Gene Woodling, and more good pitchers than could be stuffed onto an average playing squad. And Ol' Case handled them *his* way, knowing every ache and pain that afflicted any of them, playing no favorites, shifting positions to gain greater power, making heroes by the dozen because "The Perfessor" had the right idea at the right instant. He began with the Yankees as Manager of the Year; he ended his twelve-year reign as the Yankee pilot in 1961 as Manager of the Century. Comparisons were inevitable:

In 30 years with the Giants, crabby John McGraw had won 10 National League pennants and 3 World Series.

125

In 50 years with the Philadelphia Athletics, gentle Connie Mack had won 9 American League pennants and 5 World Series.

In 15-plus years with the Yankees, cold-minded Joe McCarthy had won 8 American League pennants and 7 World Series.

In 12 years with the Yankees, fighting little Miller Huggins had won 6 American League pennants and 3 World Series.

And under "nutsy" Ol' Case? In 12 years with the Yankees, Stengel won 10 American League pennants and 9 World Series (in 1960, the Pirates finally beat him in the seventh game). Baseball had never known such a manager; his equal is not yet in sight.

But Casey was now seventy and the Yankees, considering the old man played out, did not renew his contract. New Yorkers — even those not dedicated to the Yankees — were infuriated. "My services were no longer desired," said Ol' Case, which only added fuel to the fire.

"He is secure in a first place of affection for the pleasure he has given us all through these many years," editorialized *The New York Times* in a tribute that had begun almost tearfully: "The New Yorker's heart is heavy with the departure of Casey Stengel."

For once, *The New York Times* had misread history. Ol' Case was not through with New York City. At the appropriate moment he would return — with a bang — in his own "nutsy" way.

* * * *

Baseball's charm has always been the unexpected. Doubtless when in 1875 Joseph E. Brown pitched the Philadelphia Nationals to a no-hit victory over Chicago, fans believed they had witnessed a "miracle," and when the following season Borden, pitching for Boston, fashioned another no-hitter, 8 to 0, over Cincinnati, a baseball millenium may have seemed the result. But thereafter no-hitters would pile up, season after season. Old-timers who (depending on their age) measured pitching immortals by the names of Christy Mathewson, Grover Cleveland Alexander, Walter Johnson and Carl Hubbell would learn that nothing is unique in baseball. The unbelievable grows out of the fact that better child care, nutrition and scientific knowledge produce athletes who go on to more astonishing triumphs.

126

No one could argue with Carl Hubbell when he wrote his "ten commandments" for pitching success:

1. A limber arm.
2. A rugged physique, or, as an alternative, wiriness.
3. A repertoire, meaning a fast ball and at least one breaking ball, preferably a curve.
4. Control.
5. Competitive courage.
6. Endurance.
7. Intelligence.
8. The ability to size up a hitter.
9. Confidence.
10. Fielding skill.

Sandy Koufax, who just possibly may be the greatest pitcher baseball ever has known, would agree with all of these requirements for a successful hurler. But Sandy would have said all this a bit differently:

"I start every game with the hope of pitching a no-hitter. After the first hit, I'm trying for a one-hitter. If I lose a shutout, then I try to pitch a one-run game."

Brooklyn-born, Sandy gravitated naturally to the Dodgers in those years when "the Bums," under Walter Alston, were becoming a power in the National League. Sandy possessed everything a pitcher could want: a blazing fast ball, an eye-blinking curve, a deceptive change-up. Not in a century had any National Leaguer topped 300 strikeouts; in 1963, when as a 25-game winner Sandy helped carry the Dodgers to the pennant, he struck out 306. So fans began to talk records: about Howard Ehmke of the Philadelphia Athletics, who had struck out 13 Chicago Cubs in the 1929 World Series; about Carl Erskine, who had struck out 14 Yankees in the 1953 World Series. Could Sandy beat 'em both for a new mark?

Sixty thousand fans packed the Stadium for the opening game in 1963. Alston went with Koufax for his starter; the indomitable Whitey Ford, a lifetime winner of ten World Series games, was the inevitable Yankee choice. For Sandy the going promised to be tough. Mickey Mantle, who had been brought up to the Yankees to replace Joe DiMaggio in center field, could hit the ball a country mile. There was Roger Maris, who had hit 61 home runs in 1961 to break Ruth's old record. And there were others in the Yankee line-up to brighten the eyes of the club's blond-haired manager, Ralph Houk: seasoned veterans like Elston Howard and Tony Kubek, Bobby Richardson and Joey Pepitone. Before the afternoon ended, Houk expected, the nation would know how much pitching ability supported the nickname of "Sandy the Dandy."

The first inning was scoreless (with two strikeouts for Ford, three for Sandy). The Stadium was in an uproar. Whitey opened the second by enticing Tommy Davis, a dangerous hitter, to ground out.

Sandy Koufax of the Los Angeles Dodgers, "winningest" major-league pitcher of 1966, and Eddie Mathews of the Atlanta Braves seem to be performing an unrehearsed soft-shoe dance during this game. Mathews was subsequently put out after being caught off base. (Pleading a recurring disability in his pitching arm, Sandy retired from baseball as a player at the end of the 1966 season.)

Sandy Koufax winds up for a fast delivery.

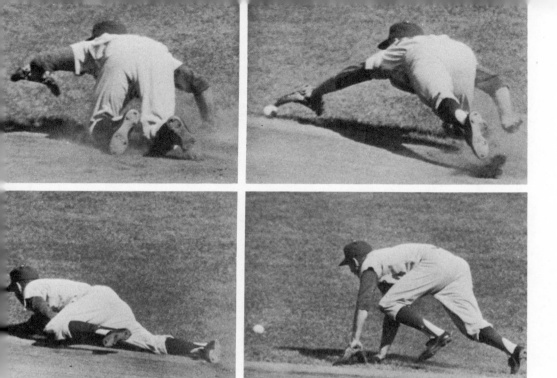

The first game of the 1963 World Series resulted in the defeat of the Yankees by the Dodgers, 5 to 2. The sequence photos above show Dick Tracewski, Los Angeles second baseman, scrambling to get ball hit by Clete Boyer of the Yankees in the fifth inning. Boyer was credited with a single.

The ball stayed fair and went all the way for a Yankee home run during this game between the Dodgers and the Yankees in the 1963 World Series. Questions: (1) Which spectators are Yankee fans? (2) Which one is the Dodger fan?

Whitey looked his customary cocky self, plucking at his shirt front — and then calamity stalked into the stadium. Frank Howard doubled — a faster runner would have made it to third; Bill Skowron, a one-time Yankee, singled; Dick Tracewski, no better than a utility second baseman, dropped a fly safely into center; and then catcher Johnny Roseboro, blinking through his eyeglasses, slashed down the right-field foul line a hit that delights sportscasters as they scream, "If she stays fair, she's a goner." "She" stayed fair for nearsighted Roseboro, and that homer put the Dodgers out in front, 4 to 0. The fifth run that the Dodgers added in the fifth inning actually was not important; nor, really, were the two runs that the Yankees scored in the eighth; for when this game reached two outs in the ninth, Sandy had racked up 14 strikeouts and stood only one away from World Series immortality.

The crowd, the press were with Sandy. At the plate stood Harry Bright, a pinch-hitter. Everyone moaned when Bright dribbled a ball down the third base line; then, as the ball rolled foul, a huge sigh swept over the Stadium. Sandy still had a chance! With the count at 2-and-2, Harry Bright dug in at the plate, grim, determined. He saw Sandy go into his stretch. He saw Sandy's strong left arm sweep downward. He saw the ball streak, meteor-like, toward the plate. Harry Bright swung mightily. A shout of joy shook the ranks of Dodger and Yankee fans alike — Harry Bright had struck out! It made scant difference that four days later Sandy again beat the Yankees, 2 to 1. It almost did not matter that the Dodgers took the World Series from the Yankees four games in a row, in itself something of an unprecedented feat. The unforgettable moment was that last pitch against Harry Bright in the first game. Baseball without new heroes? What sort of national pastime would *that* be?

Turnabout is fair play. Actress Doris Day autographs a baseball for the Yankee "home-run twins," Roger Maris (left) and Mickey Mantle (right). The occasion was the completion of a scene in a Hollywood movie, made in 1961, in which the baseball players portrayed themselves. (Roger Maris was traded by the Yankees at the end of the 1966 season.)

Those Amazing Mets

A Willie Mays whaling the ball over the wall, a Casey Stengel tipping his cap while a sparrow flew out, a Sandy Koufax fanning fifteen Yankees in a World Series opener supply the thrills and chuckles of the game that the fans remember. But, essentially, baseball remains a business that cannot survive without changes that sometimes infuriate the customers.

When Warren Crandall Giles took over from Ford Frick as president of the National League, this wily baseball man knew that the Boston Braves were in serious trouble. In 1948 — a pennant-winning year for the Braves — the home attendance had totaled 1,455,431; by 1952, this figure had dropped to 281,278, and the club's financial loss was $600,000. On March 13, 1953 — called Black Friday in Boston — the bitter news broke: league owners had agreed to moving the Boston franchise to Milwaukee.

Here beautiful new Milwaukee County Stadium and 1,826,397 screaming, admission-paying Wisconsin fans awaited the Braves. Giles answered his critics blandly: "I have never heard a major-league club owner or official express a view that a city which has the physical ability to support big-league ball should be deprived of it."

Other, more revolutionary changes were in the wind. When in 1956 the Dodgers played eight home games in Jersey City, New Jersey, their strong-minded president, Walter O'Malley, was serving serious warning: either his Dodgers must be given larger playing grounds or the team would wave good-by to Brooklyn. Then O'Malley sold Ebbets Field to a real estate promoter and purchased the Los Angeles franchise in the Pacific Coast League. Dodger fans wailed to the heavens, calling O'Malley, in moments of restraint, the twentieth-century Judas; and Gladys Gooding, the club's organist, played plaintively, "Say It Isn't So."

Nor was this the end of the sacrilege for poor little ol' New York. In two years, from 1954 to 1956, the home attendance of the Giants

131

had declined from 1,155,067 to 629,179, and without any show of crocodile tears, their president, Horace Stoneham, told the press: "I feel bad about the kids. I've seen lots of them at the Polo Grounds. But I haven't seen many of their fathers lately."

So the Giants (with Willie Mays) were bound for San Francisco. Dodger and Giant fans, once locked in the great camaraderie of eternal hatred, now embraced in common grief. But a single year proved the business wisdom behind these switches: in 1957, the total home attendance of the National League was 8,819,701; in 1958, this figure jumped to 10,164,596.

But happier days were ahead, although they would not arrive until the 1962 season, when both leagues expanded to ten teams, adding Los Angeles (now called California) and Kansas City to the American League and Houston and New York to the National.*

Was New York ready for the return of National League baseball, even if it had to start in the rattrap the old Polo Grounds now had become? Was Noah ready for the Ark? With almost as queer an assort-

Shea Stadium, home of the New York Mets, as it appeared on April 16, 1964, one day before the Mets' inaugural game there. In the background are World's Fair buildings, also nearing completion.

(Opposite page) The lights of Shea Stadium, estimated at an output of two million watts and reportedly the best ever constructed, go on officially for the first time in a night game between the Mets and the Cincinnati Reds, May 6, 1964.

*Dwindling home attendance led in 1966 to the transfer of the Milwaukee franchise to Atlanta.

ment as that with which the Biblical gentleman had loaded his craft, the New York Mets burst upon the city and the nation.

Daffy? No team, no group of fans in the entire history of the game, ever approached such daffiness. The "man in the gray flannel suit" who rooted for the Yankees, as Robert M. Lipsyte pointed out in *The New York Times,* would never comprehend the Metaphile who went crazy over a team that won 40 games (never more than three in a row) and lost 120 games in 1962. No one could understand why this "new breed" of baseball nut had developed. The aloof *New Yorker's* analyst decided that there was "more Met than Yankee in every one of us"; Charles Collingwood decided on CBS that "the Mets are the beneficiaries of the Underdog Factor, a powerful nutriment in the building of loyalty"; Red Smith decided that such an *aficionado* was the spurned victim of O'Malley's Gold Rush to Los Angeles. Met fans were teenagers mostly, kids carrying signs that read, "Our Mom Loves the Mets"; or another reading:

"M is for Mighty
E is for Exciting
T is for Terrific
S is for So Lovable."

Ol' Case, called back to New York to manage the Mets, as bright in his 70's as he had been when masterminding the fabulous Yankees in his 60's, understood both the "road apples" on his squad and the "nutsy" crowd that adored some of the worst ball players the game had ever produced. In two words — a baseball record for Ol' Case — he explained the entire phenomenon:

"They're amazin'."

*　　*　　*　　*

Once, after the Mets had thrown away a ball game in a manner completely unimaginable, Casey sat alone in the dugout, moaning: "I keep tellin' myself I'm dreamin' these terrible things that happen. But I ain't."

At the opening of spring training in St. Petersburg, Florida, Casey pulled a ball from his hip pocket and announced to the Mets squad: "Now this is a baseball." He pointed out the locations of the three bases

Casey Stengel, first manager of the New York Mets, applies an ice bag to his head to combat the effects of summer heat and some plays made by his team.

"Marvelous Marv" Throneberry reaches high, but can't quite glove the wild throw from Frank Thomas of the Mets. Runner reaching first base is St. Louis Cardinals' pitcher Bob Gibson.

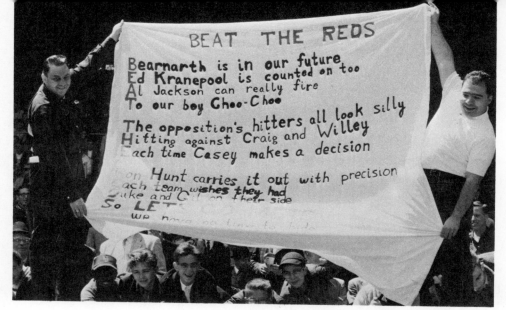

The "new breed" of baseball fans in New York, ever anxious to display their loyalty and devotion to the Mets in unmistakable terms, would whip up banners such as this one at the drop of a ball.

and home plate. Then he trudged back to the bench, hoping something would turn out right. It rarely did, causing Casey once to advise his outfielders: "When you field a grounder, throw the ball to third — that way you can hold a single to a double!" But the Mets had one high moment that spring; they beat the Yankees, 4 to 3.

The symbol of the team, as the season spun out its horrors, became Throneberry, known to the Mets' faithful as "Marvelous Marv." Throneberry was the type of player who would chase down a runner between first and second, unmindful of the runner on third, who meanwhile scampered home with the winning run: Marv possessed an almost matchless talent for losing games while he "thought through" plays. The Mets lost their first nine games; later, they would break that streak by dropping 11 in a row, which seemed like a feat that should stand off all challengers; but a 17-game losing streak followed — the Mets had a grip like a lobster's claw on last place.

But the fans who poured into the Polo Grounds adored their clownish heroes; they came night and day, shattering attendance records;

an occasional victory produced delirium, if not as many barrels of joyful tears as Rheingold was selling through the stands. They adored bugging Marvelous Marv: "If you weren't so old, you'd be a great Little League player!"; they devoted hours to painting signs that they paraded around the Polo Grounds — signs that read, "Cranbury, Strawberry, We Love Throneberry" and "Let's Go Mets" and "Mike's Diner Digs the Mets," among thousands of others. To the Mets' owners, baseball might remain a business, but to Met fans it had become the greatest show on earth.

A moment of wild exultation came at Yankee Stadium in 1963, where the Mets and Yankees competed for the Mayor's Trophy in an exhibition game designed to benefit sandlot baseball around New York City. A roar of 50,000 greeted the Mets as they trotted onto the field, but underneath there was a seething discontent. Staid Stadium cops took away the beloved Mets signs at the gates, as though such declarations as "O'Malley Is a Fink" and "Off the Floor in '64" were beneath Yankee dignity.

But the cops missed the firecrackers, nor could they frisk the faithful of their competitive spirit — this was going to be a Mets night. Fist fights broke out all over the place. Firecrackers, artfully tossed, exploded under the feet of umpires. An effort to tear down the Yankees' championship banner was only abandoned after a furious scuffle. Rockets soared over home plate, the pitcher's mound, exploding in clouds of smoke.

And to add to the hilarity, the Mets won the game, 6 to 2. Ralph Houk, the Yankee manager, and his players stayed in the clubhouse an extra hour, believing the counsel of worried friends:

"You'll get mobbed out there!"

With Met fans chanting, "Yankees, go home!" the advice was not amiss.

*   *   *   *

The Mets began their second year almost as badly as the first — they lost eight games in a row — then they beat Milwaukee, 5 to 4, and went on to make their opening season record 8 out of 12. The mother in Demarest, New Jersey, who had offered to teach the Mets baseball in a game with her Cub Scout Troop No. 186 was forgotten (if not forgiven). Ol' Case, to the undying mystery of the kids who still strolled the Polo Grounds in their Marv T-shirts, had shipped Marvelous Marv off to the Mets farm club in Buffalo. Throneberry fans arranged to bring Marv back and land him by helicopter behind first base; a gentleman representing the Marvelous Marv Throneberry Fan Club of West New York, New Jersey, told Casey that the reason Marv "can't hit in Buffalo" was because "he's affected by the cold winds up there"; but Casey's mail by now included everything from snake charms and mystic powders for strengthening the arms of his pitchers to very sensible advice on how outfielder Frank Thomas could find his way into a sacred shrine: "He [Thomas] takes a bus to Utica, changes for a bus to Cooperstown, walks down the main street until he gets to the Hall of Fame, walks up the stairs and buys a 50-cent admission ticket at the door."

So Marvelous Marv was gone? The Mets never lacked for a hero — young or ailing — that was their magic. They had pitcher Carleton Willey, who finished his first season with the Mets winning 9 and losing 14 — a good-enough record on a last-place club for him to be named Rookie of the Year. They had Craig Anderson, a really good hurler, who managed a streak of 18 straight losses (very few of which were his fault with this very bad ball club). They had Eddie Kranepool — an $80,000-bonus kid out of James Monroe High School in the Bronx of New York — who after seasoning in the minors (Syracuse, Knoxville, Auburn) proved worth the faith invested in him. They had Rod Kanehl, after whom two gentlemen, writing on stationery of the Monmouth(N. J.) Park Race Track, wanted to name a horse. And they had the aging Duke Snider, now gray around the temples and bending a bit at the knees, who told fans that the Dodgers never should have been moved out of Brooklyn. The Mets needed nothing more — youth with hope, age with love, a sport above a business, talkative Ol' Case who could not shut up any more than he could fall asleep at night — heck, the Mets were ready to remake baseball as a national pastime, and, in their own way, succeeded.

Daffy New York fans acquired a new home in 1964 with the construction of Shea Stadium on Long Island's Flushing Meadows.

Named in honor of William A. Shea, an attorney and prime mover in returning organized baseball to New York, this spectacular sports arena possessed escalators and elevators that helped to carry more than 50,000 Met fanatics to three tiers of seats. Not a single pillar impeded the viewing of any Met error — baseball's most imperfect team had the nation's most perfect playing field. There were 45 acres of parking space for cars; the subway and the Long Island Rail Road rumbled up to the turnstiles. And Ol' Case, who must have been infected by Marvelous Marv, made a remarkable television address. Ol' Case, rambling on through sentences that started, intertwined, never ended, like a Met outfielder chasing a rebounding fly, thanked Ballantine beer for its advertising sponsorship of the Met games. Afterward the truth was whispered to Casey: Rheingold beer sponsored the Mets.

But who cared?

Once each year the Mets have a parade of all sign painters who love the team. Weeks, months go into designing these tokens of love. Oldsters who once lived their lifetimes at Ebbets Field, rooting for the Dodgers, or old-time Giant fans from the Polo Grounds, showed up among the more than two thousand marchers who appeared in the 1966 parade. Kids — toddlers, really — were there, with their fathers and mothers and sisters and brothers, helping them carry their handiwork. "Wait until next year!" the once-perennial cry of the lovers of the Dodgers, never could equal in the hope of the faithful one sign carried that afternoon:

"Would you believe 1999?"

Afterward the Met players came out of the dugout. They stood around the infield, each holding a card with a single letter. Together they spelled:

TO THE METS FANS —
WE LOVE YOU, TOO!

The New York Mets have created a new problem in baseball. Is it a sport or a business or a love affair?

In 1966, the incomparable Casey Stengel, amid flowing thousands of words, had left the Mets to manage his banking interests in and about Glendale, California. A new manager, Wes Westrum, had carried the Mets to more than fifty victories in August and they were solidly

(Above) View of Houston's Astrodome Stadium, as it neared completion in the summer of 1964. (Right) Casey Stengel pauses for a fond farewell look at Shea Stadium after retiring as manager of the Mets in 1965.

in ninth place ahead of the Chicago Cubs, now managed by an old lover of baseball glad to be back in a uniform and spiked shoes, Leo Durocher.

Houston's Astrodome, glass-enclosed to provide cover in all kinds of weather, may be one answer to baseball in the Jet Age. Old guys coming and going, a Stengel or a Durocher, may be another, because a fan forgives. The game has never belonged to the managers or the owners, but to eternal youth:

"Would you believe 1999?"

In an editorial entitled, "The Year of the Mets," *The New York Times* commented on the 1966 season:

"The Yankees ended up in last place for the first time since 1912; and the Mets didn't — for the first time ever. It is of mere academic interest that the Yanks actually won more games and finished closer to first place in the American League than the Mets did in the National. What counts is that in the National League, the Chicago Cubs were worse."

But *The Times* also could foresee possible trouble for the Mets:

"... Now that they are just another thoroughly professional second division club, the fans may demand even better performances: eighth place, then seventh — there is no limit to rising expectations. But for the moment, ninth place is the top of the world."

* * * *

In 1966, that immortal year when the Amazin' Mets moved out of the National League cellar, the Los Angeles Dodgers met the Baltimore Orioles in the World Series. Traditionally, because of the tensions involved, such games rarely are well played, but the Dodgers broke records that had stood for half a century. Not since 1905, when the mighty Joe McGinnity and Christy Mathewson of the New York Giants combined their remarkable talents to hold the Philadelphia Athletics to twenty-eight scoreless innings in a row, would any team approach the marvelous record of the Dodgers in going thirty-three consecutive innings without scoring a run.

Shown here is one of the errors that contributed to the defeat of the Dodgers by the Baltimore Orioles in the 1966 World Series. Jim Gilliam (19), Dodger third baseman, moves away from the bag to take the wild throw of right fielder Ron Fairly as Baltimore's Boog Powell (26) lumbers into third. Umpire is Mel Steiner.

Dodger shortstop Maury Wills takes to the air to get off his throw to first base. Sliding out is Curt Blefary of the Orioles. Umpire is Cal Drummond.

140

Other festive feats of ineptitude were compiled by the Dodgers: most errors in an inning — three (the handiwork of Willie Davis, a really fine centerfielder); most strikeouts by a relief pitcher — eleven (achieved by Moe Drabowsky of the Orioles, who was brought in to cool off the Dodgers after they had scored two runs, their total run-production for the series); most errors in one game — six (another Dodger accomplishment which contrasted poorly with the 1.000 per cent fielding performance of the Orioles in winning four straight games); and there were still other records established by the Dodgers to perplex their faithful followers. Their team batting percentage of .142 was a new low in World Series competition (the Orioles hit only .200, which scarcely shook baseball's long history). But the Dodgers soared to other heights: making the fewest total hits in a series (17), the fewest total bases (24, including 14 singles, 3 doubles, 1 home run), and the "fewest" of everything else.

The city — Baltimore — that had given birth to the verses of "Casey at the Bat" was overjoyed by its triumph. Another Casey — Ol' Case Stengel — could have said more simply what thousands of sports writers tried to explain, for The Perfessor might have said of the Dodgers what he said of the Mets in their first season:

"They're amazin'."

Third baseman Brooks Robinson of the Baltimore Orioles is greeted by the outstretched hands of his teammates as he returns to the dugout after slugging his first-inning home run in the opening game of the 1966 World Series.

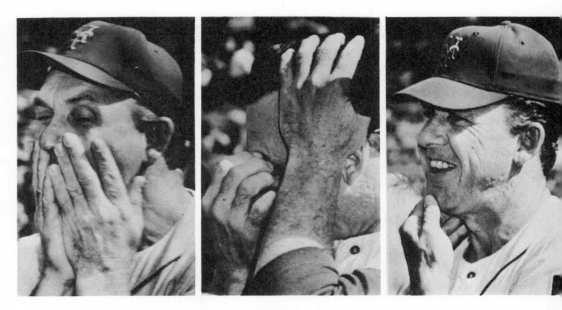

Gil Hodges, manager of the New York Mets, reflects the almost unendurable heart-pounding emotions of thousands of his team's fans during World Series play.

The Name of the Game

The year 1969 marked the Centennial Anniversary of professional baseball. A sense of change and rebellion was in the air. Fans who did not wish to have the game lose its status as the "national pastime" against such oncoming powerful professional sports as football, basketball and auto racing were sharply critical of such rule changes as lowering the pitching mound and lessening the size of the strike zone in an effort to give the batter dominance over the pitcher.

A good share of the trouble stemmed from the fact that not one fan or player in ten really knew anything about Bowie Kuhn, baseball's new commissioner. What did he understand about the game? Generally, however, fans approved of the plan to expand the major leagues to twenty-four teams, although there were also numerous scowls as they examined the new team groupings (in the order in which they finished at the end of the season):

142

AMERICAN LEAGUE	NATIONAL LEAGUE
Eastern Division	**Eastern Division**
Baltimore	New York
Detroit	Chicago
Boston	Pittsburgh
Washington	St. Louis
New York	Philadelphia
Cleveland	Montreal
Western Division	**Western Division**
Minnesota*	Atlanta*
Oakland	San Francisco
California*	Cincinnati
Kansas City	Los Angeles
Chicago	Houston
Seattle	San Diego

The scowlers were worried over the divisional split between the leagues, which demanded a play-off of three games out of five before each league winner could grapple in the four-games-out-of-seven struggle for the World Championship. To the scowlers it all seemed like too much post-season baseball. Yet there was very little disagreement when on the evening of the 40th All-Star Game at the Baseball Centennial Dinner four players were elevated to sports immortality:

Babe Ruth — "The Greatest Player Ever."

John J. McGraw — "The Greatest Manager Ever."

Joe DiMaggio — "The Greatest Living Player." (Willie Mays was a close second choice.)

Casey Stengel — "The Greatest Living Manager."

*   *   *   *

---

*Minnesota actually represented the "twin cities" of St. Paul and Minneapolis; Atlanta seemed misplaced, but the team had taken over the franchise of the old Milwaukee Braves; California, playing in Anaheim, figuratively sat on the back doorstep of the Los Angeles Dodgers.

Old "Case," as manager, had parted company from "The Amazin' Mets," preferring less strenuous activity in his waning years, while the Mets, in 1966 and 1968, broke tradition by finishing one notch *above* last place. The manager now was Gil Hodges, who had handled the Washington Senators two years before with quiet effectiveness. The previous fall he had suffered a heart attack, casting some doubt over whether he could endure another season with any team, especially the Mets.

As the 1969 season opened, "smart-money" gamblers in Las Vegas offered odds of 100 to 1 against the Mets finishing first in the Eastern Division of the National League. Chicago, taking the lead on opening day and holding it as mid-August approached, turned that city's North Side into near-bedlam. A band of young rooters, known in Wrigley Field as the Bleacher Bums, led the howls for the Cubs to steal home with as many pennants as existed — divisional, league and World Championship. About this time the Mets had climbed to third place, 9½ games behind Chicago. Then, like Alice in Lewis Carroll's classic, they found the rabbit's hole that would lead them to Wonderland. They jumped in.

The sports writers, like many a fan who lived outside Metsville (as New York was soon called), could not really believe what they saw and read. One claimed that Hodges' team had graduated from being amazin' and had gone into the realm of the supernatural. "God made the Mets," declared one of the team's coaches. "Then He became our Number One fan."

* * * *

Suddenly the Mets could not lose for winning. Youth was on their side (first baseman Ed Kranepool was the only player remaining from Casey's original team) — and youthful exuberance was not easily daunted. A newscaster, seeing two slim infielders, Bud Harrelson and Al Weis, standing together in their uniforms, asked: "Hey, what happened to you guys — miss the bus to a Little League game?"

Harrelson and Weis simply grinned — they had been kidded this way before. Sometimes their sparkling infield play made fans believe

Tom Seaver's wind-up of a pitch that has proven to be the nemesis of many an opposing batter.

they were the spark plugs of this unstoppable Mets team. But any number of players could have been singled out for distinction: pitchers such as young Tom Seaver, the only 25-game winner of baseball's centennial, and Jerry Koosman, who had been recommended by a stadium usher and signed for a pittance bonus of $1,200. Or outfielders like Tom Agee and Cleon Jones, boyhood friends from Mobile, Alabama, who clouted home runs when they were needed and made catches that were fantastically spectacular. Or catchers like Jerry Grote, who had made the All-Star team in '68. Or coaches like Yogi Berra, who

145

had been catcher for the Yankees for 18 years and who possessed a lifetime record of 358 home runs.

Somehow, individual stars did not seem to represent the Mets in Wonderland. When one player had an off-day, another merely picked up the slack. That was their true secret: they played like a high-spirited *team,* as skillfully put together as a finely jeweled watch. At the beginning of the season Gil Hodges had predicted his team would win 85 games. The Mets did better, scoring an even hundred victories and beating out Chicago for the National League's Eastern Division title by eight games.

Baltimore had won the Eastern Division title in the American League by nineteen games and Minnesota had prevailed in the Western Division by nine games. Not to be outdone by the Mets, Baltimore also swept the AL play-offs by scores of 5-4 (in 12 innings), 1-0 and 11-2. Reputedly Baltimore possessed the most powerful team in organized baseball, as Frank Robinson, the Orioles' slugging outfielder who sometimes was called "Motor-mouth," happily explained to anyone willing to listen. Baltimore was superior in pitching, hitting, fielding and base-running. In short, the Orioles would chew the Mets into mincemeat.

Naturally, the odds-makers agreed. But others did not. One was Old Case, who in a perfect example of Stengelese that required a scholar to unscramble, declared: "The team has come along slow but fast." Another was New York's Mayor John Lindsay, who, with apologies to *Casey at the Bat,* ended an *Ode to the New York Mets* with these lines:

> So good luck down in Baltimore — New Yorkers, place your bets.
> We know we've got a winner — with our Amazin' Mets.

In the opening game of the World Series, Tom Seaver, now credited with eleven victories in a row, gave Don Buford, Oriole left fielder, a home run on the second pitch of the game. Cuban-born Mike Cuellar, a 20-game winner, seemed to weave a spider's web around Mets batters. By the fourth inning, when Baltimore scored three runs, it was clear to the more than 50,000 in the stands that Tom was still "too loose." Relief pitchers held Baltimore scoreless throughout the remainder of what the Associated Press called "a routine game." The only bit of face-saving for the Mets came in the seventh when two

146

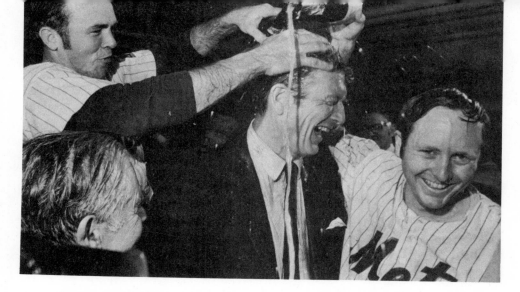

Jerry Grote (left) and Rod Gaspar (right) shower champagne upon New York's mayor shortly after the Mets clinched the National League pennant. It was but a preliminary celebration. Ten days later the Mets were World Champions.

singles and a walk enabled Al Weis to drive in a run — the first scored on Baltimore in 39 innings of World Championship play (the Orioles defeated the Los Angeles Dodgers on four straight shutouts in 1966).

This 4-to-1 victory brought another 50,000-plus crowd to watch Baltimore continue the slaughter. Hodges sent his left-hander, Koosman, against Dave McNally, a 20-game winner. As a kid, Koosman had dreamed of pitching a no-hit, no-run game in the World Series, and for six innings the dream endured. Meanwhile, the Mets scored on a homer by Donn Clendenon, a six-foot, three-inch first baseman who came to New York from Montreal on a trade in June. That home run, matched by Harrelson's sparkling infield play, held up until the seventh, when Baltimore scored. Singles placed Mets on first and third two innings later as Al Weis came to bat. Even though Weis had driven in New York's one run the previous day, Baltimore did not take him seriously. After all, he had only hit .215 during the regular season. Quiet and diffident, and called "the Silent Met," Weis hit McNally's first pitch, a slider, for a single to left, and Ed Charles, a thirty-seven-year-old utility third baseman, romped home with the run that won the game for the Mets, 2-1, and evened the series.

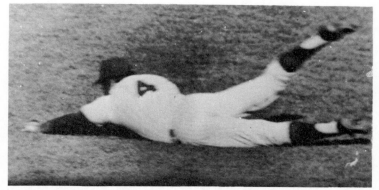

Sensational catches contributed no little to the well-earned victory of the 1969 World Championship Mets. (Above) With the bases full of Orioles, Mets center-fielder Tom Agee goes into an effective acrobatic routine as he captures and holds on to a ball driven his way by Paul Blair. It made for a third out. (Right) Ron Swoboda makes a diving catch of Brooks Robinson's line drive, rolls over, and holds up the ball.

148

Fifty-six thousand Metsomaniacs jammed Shea Stadium for the third game. Hodges sent Gary Gentry back to pitch against Baltimore's talented Jim Palmer. Gentry lasted for 6⅔ innings before he tired, but by then the Mets led, 4 to 0. Sensational catches by Tommy Agee robbed the Orioles of six, and perhaps seven, runs. Gentry would have to share the day's honors with Agee, who also slammed in a home run. Ed Kranepool's homer in the eighth sweetened the 5-to-0 victory that found screaming Mets fans gloating: "Two more to go!"

The fourth game stretched ten innings. At last Tom Seaver was back in form, though he owed much to his defensive support. An example of "Mets Magic" was Ron Swoboda's diving, swanlike catch of a sinking line drive that robbed Baltimore's Brooks Robinson of an extra base hit. A crowd exceeding 57,000 howled their delight. A home run by Clendenon in the second held up as Seaver added eight more to Baltimore's string of unhappy, scoreless innings. But then the sagging Orioles appeared to regain their wind when Frank Robinson scored in the ninth. But the Mets were not to be denied and could thank Oriole blunders on a pinch bunt by J[oseph] C[lifton] Martin. The Baltimore catcher, throwing the ball, struck the hitter. The ball bounced off into a rattled Baltimore infield, allowing Rod Gaspar, a utility outfielder playing his first year with the varsity, to rush in with the run that gave the Mets their third Series triumph, 2 to 1.

So now it was only "one to go," and even the odds-makers switched to the Mets to win the championship. Koosman pitched the final game and was badly shaken by three Oriole runs in the third. But the Mets never faltered either on defense or at bat in this crisis. Clendenon hit his second home run in two days, and slender Al Weis the seventh in his seven years in the majors, as the Mets forged to the front, 5 to 3.

*   *   *   *

Shea Stadium went wild. Thousands of fans jumped onto the field as the pandemonious ovation to the Mets gained momentum. When the bases quickly disappeared, other Met partisans tore up clumps of turf for souvenirs until Shea Stadium soon resembled a battlefield rather than a baseball park. The only comment Mrs. Joan Payson, owner of the Mets, could make upon the fact that her team was now World Champions was "Oh, my! Oh, my!"

The excitement spread throughout the city. From Wall Street to midtown Manhattan, tons of ticker tape, pages torn from telephone books, computer cards and paper streamers snowed down on streets already jammed with people who had given up all thought of further business that day. A jubilant Madison Avenue bus driver greeted passengers with the shout: "Everyone rides free!" Commented the noted violinist, Isaac Stern: "If the Mets can win in the Series, anything can happen — even peace!" Voices grew husky, if not mute, as the cry raced throughout the city: "We're Number One!" Fears were expressed that the enthusiasm would fade away before the arrival of the day officially set for a ticker-tape parade down Broadway to City Hall, among other festivities.

Such apprehensions were wasted. The crowds, if possible, were larger and more enthusiastic. Actually, as underdogs who had achieved the unbelievable, the Mets had rabid rooters in all fifty states. And the reason was understandable:

The Mets had returned baseball to the Union as its national pastime.

Wall Street typified many another New York street on the afternoon of October 16, 1969, as the Mets attained the impossible dream of becoming World Champions in baseball. A shower of paper from tall buildings seemed to be the most natural way of expressing the heights of joy and jubilation.

In 1970 both teams reached the World Series in whirlwind finishes. The Baltimore Orioles defeated the Western Division winners, the Minnesota Twins, in three straight defeats to win the American League title and the Cincinnati Reds humbled the Pittsburgh Pirates in a similar manner in winning the honors in the National League.

The extraordinary fielding and batting of the Orioles' third baseman, Brooks Robinson, would be the hero of the World Series as Baltimore crushed the Reds, four games to one. Brooks hit three home runs during the five-game contest, including two in the fifth game when Baltimore nipped Cincinnati, 6 to 5.

Actually, 1970 was a season of triumph and sorrow among individual players. Willie Mays of the San Francisco Giants and Hank Aaron of the Atlanta Braves both passed 3,000 hits and more than 500 home runs in their long careers as outfielders (Mays ended 1970 with 3,065 hits and 628 home runs, Aaron with 3,110 hits and 592 home runs).

But the year was fraught with strife. Dennis McLain, a Cy Young winner as the American League's best pitcher in 1968 and 1969, was three times suspended by Commissioner Bowie Kuhn—for an alleged involvement with gamblers, for soaking reporters with ice water, and for carrying a concealed weapon to a game in Detroit. The financial difficulties of the Seattle Club were solved by selling its option to Milwaukee.

Still, the great "headache" of 1970 was the suit of Curt Flood for $4.1 million after he had been traded to the Philadelphia Phillies from the St. Louis Cardinals. Curt challenged as "peonage and involuntary servitude" that clause in his contract which gave him no control over whether he could be sold or traded to another club. Curt gave up a reputed salary of $90,000 to carry on his fight. Commissioner Kuhn ruled against Curt and so also did Judge Irving Ben Cooper: "Clearly the preponderance of credible proof does not favor elimination of the reserve clause. Baseball remains exempt from the anti-trust laws unless and until the Supreme Court or Congress rule to the contrary." Thus the Curt Flood suit was left open to judicial appeal. Meanwhile, on the understanding he was not prejudicing his case, Curt accepted a one-year contract for $110,000 to play for the Washington Senators.

*　　*　　*　　*

As leaders of the Eastern Division, Baltimore won the American League pennant from the Oakland Athletics, Western Division victors. In the National League the eastern Pittsburgh humbled San Francisco, the pride of the West.

Hunger shone in the eyes of Pittsburgh fans who had waited eleven years to win a World Series. A sizzling series went the full seven games. Baltimore won the first two contests by the comfortable scores of 5 to 3 and 11 to 3. The Pirates bounced back, 5 to 1, and its hero was first baseman Bob Robertson who hit a three-run homer in the seventh inning. In the next game Baltimore again suffered a disastrous seventh when three consecutive singles scored Robertson and won the game for Pittsburgh. A day later Pirate fans almost ascended to heaven when Nelson Briles held the Orioles to two hits in winning 4 to 0.

Baltimore tied the series, with special indebtedness to Don Buford, its left fielder, who banged two home runs in fashioning a 3-to-0 victory. A screaming crowd packed Baltimore Memorial Stadium for the finale. A home run by Roberto Clemente, right fielder, put the Pirates in front in the fourth. A single and double gave Pittsburgh another run in the eighth. The Orioles fought back gamely. Successive singles and a sacrifice moved the tying runs into scoring position, but only one crossed the plate and the Pirates had bagged the clincher, 2 to 1. Celebrating Pittsburghers left their downtown area a shambles next morning.

*   *   *   *

Those who believed there was nothing new in professional baseball were quickly disillusioned early in 1972 when for the first time in the history of the game the players struck for added pension allowances. After thirteen days a demand for $800,000 (paid from television rights to the World Series) was reduced to $500,000. Meanwhile, the players' salaries and the owners' gate receipts for the season's first eleven games were lost. Said Commissioner Kuhn sadly: "Who won? Nobody. The players suffered. The clubs suffered. Baseball suffered."

Baseball suffered also with the death by a heart attack of Gil Hodges, manager of the Mets, although everyone approved of the appointment of Yogi Berra as his successor. The payment to the Atlanta Braves' superstar, Hank Aaron, of $600,000 for the next three years made him the highest paid player in baseball and was based on the fact that Hank, who was only 38 years of age and averaged about forty home runs a year, was most likely to break Babe Ruth's all-time record of 714 home runs. Aaron had ended his 19th major-league season with 639 home runs, or 75 fewer than Ruth.

Meanwhile, Willie Mays, who had hit 648 home runs, was believed to have outlived his baseball usefulness. After playing twenty-one seasons with the Giants in New York and San Francisco, Willie signalized his personal victory against the Giants by winning his first game for the Mets with his 649th home run. As though advertising 1972 as a season in which anything could happen, Burt Hooton, a graduate of the University of Texas and a 22-year-old right-handed rookie pitcher for the Chicago Cubs, won a no-hit, no-run game from the Philadelphia Phillies, 4 to 0. Three spectacular catches, proving that baseball is still a team game, saved the triumph for Hooten. "He holds the ball like a knuckle-ball and pushes out," the Cub catcher said. "It has a spin opposite from a fastball and the ball drops down sharply when it reaches the plate."

The Oakland Athletics, spiritual heirs of the old Philadelphia Athletics under Connie Mack who had won their last world championship in 1930, demonstrated once more that all America loves an underdog. In green and gold uniforms, and the proud owners of flowing mustaches, the Oakland team appeared to have stepped from the Gay Nineties into the hearts of many of the forty million television viewers. The American League was the weaker of the two baseball leagues in 1972, and no one expected the dandified but financially unsuccessful Californians to beat out Detroit for the league title. A full five games were needed for the Athletics to win the pennant.

Meanwhile, the Cincinnati Reds had overwhelmed the world champion Pittsburgh Pirates for the National League laurels. Cincinnati was a team of superstars—Johnny Bench behind the plate, Joe Morgan at second, and Pete Rose in the outfield.

The World Series opened in the Cincinnati stadium where the artificial turf allowed balls to bounce over the heads of infielders, and when the game ended, the astonishing Oakland team had won. In fact, the Athletics jumped off to a 3-to-1 lead in games. The streets of Las Vegas, it was said, flowed with the blood of professional gamblers who had cut their throats. Among the Oakland heroes was catcher Gene Tenace, who had hit only five home runs in 1972 and now proceeded to hit four in Series competition. The relief pitching of Rollie Fingers and Vida Blue became as sensational as the hitting and ball-snagging of Joe Rudi in leftfield.

Cincinnati simply would not quit, winning the next two games (one by the score of 8 to 1, the only game of the seven won by more than one run). The World Series was tied at three games for each team, and Cincinnati, back at Riverfront Stadium with the bouncy artificial turf, was restored as the favorite. But someone forgot to make this fact known to Tenace, now called "Fury Gene," whose single and double supplied the 3-to-2 victory that the Athletics carried home to an exuberant Oakland.

*　　*　　*　　*

The suspense, excitement and jubilation of the 1972 World Series had barely subsided when the baseball world, and the world at large, was stunned to learn that the indomitable yet all-too-mortal heart of Jackie Robinson had stopped on the morning of October 24. Only nine days earlier, suffering from failing eyesight, diabetes, a cardiac condition that had developed over the years, and a pinched nerve in his leg that made walking difficult, he had been presented with an award from Baseball Commissioner Bowie Kuhn for his significant efforts against drug addiction through rehabilitation programs. The presentation had taken place just prior to the second game of the World Series in Cincinnati. The award itself was but a small measure of acknowledgment of long hours spent by him in studying and combating this insidious social problem.

Outpourings of sincere tribute to the first black player in major-league baseball (and later the first to enter the Hall of Fame) were overwhelming. President Richard Nixon—who had selected Robinson as a member of his own "all-time" baseball team—reflected the sentiments of Jackie Robinson's proudest fans with these words:

"His courage, his sense of brotherhood, and his brilliance on the playing field brought a new human dimension not only to the game of baseball but to every area of American life where black and white people work side by side. This nation, to which he gave so much in his lifetime, will miss Jackie Robinson, but his example will continue to inspire us for years to come."

154